RIDE BETTER AND BETTER

Do you wish to reach the top in competition riding? Have you a lot of riding experience, but no expert on hand to advise you?

Then this sequel to *Learn to ride well* by Josephine Pullein-Thompson is the book for you.

With the aid of many illustrations and diagrams, the author outlines clearly and carefully a course of schooling for jumping, dressage and cross country work at elementary or advanced level.

JOSEPHINE PULLEIN-THOMPSON

Ride better
and better

Illustrations by Priscilla Goodfield

KNIGHT BOOKS
Hodder & Stoughton

ISBN 0 340 20078 2

Text copyright © Josephine Pullein-Thompson
Illustrations © Blackie & Son Ltd

First published by Blackie & Son Ltd

This edition first published in 1977

Printed and bound in Great Britain in Knight Books for
Hodder & Stoughton Children's Books, a division of Hodder & Stoughton Ltd,
Arlen House, Salisbury Road, Leicester by
Richard Clay (The Chaucer Press), Ltd, Bungay, Suffolk

Contents

Introduction

This book is designed to carry on where my earlier book, *Learn to Ride Well*, finished. Its objects are to help those who can ride to ride better, to give advice on the training of horses and ponies for those who have no experienced horseman to help them, and to assist ambitious riders to achieve their ambitions.

Nothing is more depressing than working hard and getting nowhere. Many riders school with conscientious regularity but, because of some small fault in their own riding, produce either no result or, worse still, a confused and irritable horse. Others, with only the vaguest idea of their immediate aims, drift round the school boring themselves and their mounts. Some riders put up with horses or ponies that are totally unsuited to them or their purpose, others waste years trying to turn a horse into something it is incapable of becoming, and a few lay the blame for their own inadequacies on every horse they ride.

One hears riders complaining that they have not been chosen for Pony Club or riding club teams but, before they convince themselves of bias at the top, they ought to consider whether they have really developed the skills and shown the temperament and the ability to win that is necessary. One sees riders walking courses in a daze, or chattering cheerfully, with no idea what to look for or how to plan their round. One knows of those who enter for dressage tests without the least conception of how they are judged. Of course every rider expects times of depression and failure but, since life is short, one wants to make as few mistakes as possible. I hope in this book, besides helping you to improve your riding and so deepen the sympathy and strengthen the partnership between you and your horse, to minimize your failures and disappointments, and head you towards the success that anyone trying to ride better and better deserves.

1

Assessing your Ability

The best authority on your riding ability and horse management is probably your out-grown pony, and it is not a bad plan to think about the kind of reference he would give you if applied to by your new horse.

Would he say you were patient or liable to sudden rages? Bold or timid? A bit of a bully or weak and permissive? Would he recommend you as the sort of rider who makes a good partner, knowing when to take the lead and when to sit still and leave things to his horse? Or would he complain that you are a nagger, kicking continuously and to no effect? One of those busy riders, perpetually wriggling in the saddle, with hands moving and elbows and legs waving, overwhelming him with meaningless aids. That you are inclined to 'make him do it' or 'get him over' even jumps of one foot six, instead of sitting still and letting him do the actual jumping?

Or would his complaint be that you put him at jumps indecisively, not really sure whether you fancy them? That you are ignorant, and though you have walked the course you do not warn him of spreads, of hidden ditches ahead?

Would he say you were insatiably greedy, always rushing him from one show to the next with never a rest in between? Never satisfied with a clear round at home, but jumping backwards and forwards all day long over the same fences until he is driven to refusing in self-protection? Or could he say that you were a considerate rider, slowing up for deep going, avoiding over-jumping especially on hard ground, thoughtful about days off?

YOU AS A GROOM

Could he recommend your stable management? Saying that you are conscientious about clean, full water buckets, bulging haynets and well-mixed feeds—or would he have to admit that you are inclined to rush away, saying, 'You've plenty there and that water will do'?

Will he describe you as over-sentimental, pleasantly affectionate or as a rough and careless groom, brutal with the dandy brush, always pinching with the girth or banging his teeth with the bit?

Of course you can't possibly suit every pony and some of the owners of fat ponies on diets to avoid laminitis would get the most terrible stable management references, but the relationship you have had with your previous pony should be a help in deciding what sort of temperament suits you and what you will especially look for or especially avoid in the new horse. And, since a horse always needs more attention and care than a pony, do not land yourself with a bad doer unless you enjoy the cooking side of stable management. Boiling barley, making linseed mashes, grating carrots and apples onto feeds to tempt the appetite can become a burden.

YOU AS A RIDER

It is no use buying a horse which is far too good for you unless you have an instructor available to see that you do not spoil him, but on the other hand he must be better than you or you will not progress, and if he is young he must have the talent to carry you several stages further in your riding career.

If you have done a lot of competing you will know what your capabilities are. If you have won JA jumping classes on your pony you will be ready to take on a really good show-jumper, and if you have won Pony Club horse trials the move to a horse for adult Eventing is only a question of size and gaining experience of the faster speeds. But, if you have never won anything, it is better to set your sights on a horse that will win Foxhunters, or riding club horse trials rather than to try to move straight to the top.

If you have not had the opportunity to do a lot of competing how well you ride can be partly gauged by the behaviour of your out-grown pony. Is he more accomplished than when you bought him? Does he jump clear rounds over the height of which he is capable? Is his head in the right place? Is he obedient and generally co-operative, does he stand to be mounted and assist in opening gates? Could you ride a Pony Club dressage test on him? Will he turn on the forehand, rein back and shoulder-in? If you have had him for two or three years he ought to do all these things and if you have not taught him them do so at once so that you will have had some experience when it comes to teaching the new horse. Everyone makes mistakes in schooling but the more you try things out on an older horse the less chance there will be of your upsetting or spoiling your young horse. So practise riding dressage tests and attempt more advanced movements—a few steps of the turn on the haunches, a half-pass.

THE CORRECT SEAT

As well as your pony being an indicator of your riding ability there are photographs, mirrors, shop windows, instructors and even candid friends. One can judge a photograph of oneself against an illustration of the correct seat in a book and so spot one's faults, but it is better to carry a picture of the correct seat in one's mind's eye, and once you know exactly for what you are aiming the seat itself becomes far easier to acquire.

It is important to realize that the correct seat was not invented willy-nilly by some authoritarian character with a passion for rules, nor is it used only by those with a pathetic desire to conform. It is not even concerned with looking elegant; it has the severely practical purpose of seating you in a position where your weight will be least disturbing to your horse and from which you will exert maximum influence and control with minimum effort. It is designed to help you to stay with your horse through changes of speed and direction and to enable you to apply invisible aids with no time lag beyond your own reaction time.

The seat has evolved slowly over the centuries: Xenophon wrote about it some 360 years before the birth of Christ. It has

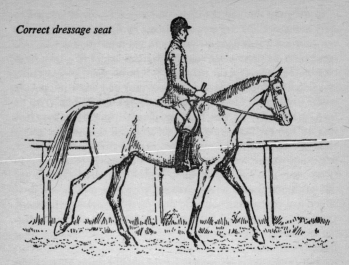

Correct dressage seat

adapted to the invention of the saddle and the stirrup, and to a lighter breed of horse. Different nations developed the seat according to their needs. The Western nations, with their wealthy aristocrats, tended towards ceremonial riding and displays in great riding houses with dressage seats, while the less civilized nations inclined towards the shorter stirrup for riding over their rougher and wilder countrysides.

The dressage seat became established in its present form during the eighteenth century, but the forward or jumping seat was invented by an Italian, Frederico Caprilli, in the early part of this century. Nowadays, there are two correct seats, but they have the same principles and rules and you can change from one to the other with only the lengthening and shortening of the stirrups as the modern horse trial rider does.

A correct seat will bring you two-thirds of the way towards becoming a good rider, but of course other attributes are necessary as well. For jumping, they would be courage, a good sense of timing, quick reactions, stamina and coolness. Slower reactions, a feeling for rhythm, calmness, perseverance, sensitivity and a concern for detail are needed for the good dressage rider. So, especially in the jumping world, you see famous riders who are successful without conforming in every way and it is sometimes tempting to copy them. Resist it. Everyone has faults, even the greatest, and by copying the more outlandish habits of great riders you will end up with their faults as well as your own. Aim for the perfect seat, and unalterable characteristics, such as being fat or thin, long backed or short armed will give you a unique style of your own in the end.

It is important to have a clear picture in one's mind of the difference between the jumping and the dressage seats. For, though the principle of the perpendicular stirrup leather and the toe never advancing beyond the knee remain the same, the shortening and lengthening of the stirrup leathers makes the two seats look very different. In the dressage seat the rider will sit erect, tall above the horse and tall below. His upper arm, the part down to the elbow, will hang by his sides, his long stirrups allow him to sink into the horse and become one with him.

In the jumping seat the shorter stirrups concertina the rider, sharpening the points of the hip, knee and ankle, causing the angles at these joints to become more acute. The rider no longer sits down, but he remains very close to the saddle and his weight, now resting on his thighs, knees and stirrups, stays just behind the horse's withers where he is strongest and so best able to carry it. It must not tip forward on the horse's neck where it would unbalance him. The rider's shoulders and hands move forward, the reins are shorter, his elbows leave his sides, but his weight must stay over the saddle. The rider is still one with his horse, anchored firmly in the position where he can be carried with least effort. He has lost some of his influence over the hindquarters of the horse, he cannot ask for collection, but he can remain balanced and with his mount at fast speeds, over rough going and large fences, through sudden changes of pace and sharp turns, without the jolts and jars and backward thrusts that he would receive if he attempted the same sort of riding with a dressage seat.

The fork seat is only possible when riding with long stirrups. It is easy to spot because the rider feels weak and inefficient and so looks unhappy. He leans forward and sometimes his toes point down and sometimes he gives the appearance of standing on tiptoe. This seat is often brought about by overkeen instructors who are determined to give their pupils a deep dressage seat immediately. But sitting deep is no use unless you can also sit tall above the horse. And the mere lengthening of stirrups does not make you sit deep; it is a matter of sinking your weight. If you feel miserable, insecure and weak when riding with long stirrups you may have a fork seat. Check with mirrors, photographs or shop windows; if you have, pull your stirrups up to the point where you feel able to keep your shoulders back. In my opinion dressage seats should be acquired gradually unless the rider can be lunged on a smooth and steady horse.

THE LEG POSITION

The correct seat depends on a correct leg position and, though, nowadays, almost everyone agrees on what is the correct leg position, it is not generally realized that a very small deviation from this position can throw out the whole seat, ruining the rider's performance and the horse's schooling especially for dressage. The rider, when sitting, must sit in the lowest part of the saddle, as close to the withers as possible, and never at the back. To allow him to do this he must have his stirrup leather under control which means that it must hang vertically, or perpendicular to the ground. With the stirrup under the ball of the foot a straight line from the point of the rider's knee to the ground should pass just in front of the toe. In other words, the rider's toe must never be in advance of his knee, not even by an eighth of an inch.

One can experiment with the evils of an incorrect leg position by pushing one's foot forward. Immediately one finds one's seat being thrust backwards in the saddle where it will cause one to be behind the movement of the horse. Being behind the movement means that instead of influencing him in a subtle manner one will obstruct and irritate him.

The heel position The heels should be down, because the rider's weight is sinking down into them. If they are forced down by pressing the feet against the stirrup the result will be a stiff knee which in turn will push the seat backwards and take the lower leg off the horse. It is very difficult to ride with a stiff knee when your stirrups are jumping length. If your pony goes far better for you when you ride short, and this is particularly apparent at the rising trot, and you do not have the success at dressage which you feel you deserve, inspect yourself critically for stiff knees. As this is not a very obvious fault it often goes undetected even by instructors, but it will make it impossible for you to turn out a well-schooled horse or ride a really good dressage test.

The toe position Another bad habit is to use the back of the lower leg for giving aids instead of the inside. The lower leg is the part below the knee and it should hang down comfortably with the feet more or less parallel to the horse. People with fat or round thighs may have to turn out their toes a little but the thin-legged should have no trouble in keeping the foot almost parallel to the horse.

Though the Victorian idea of continuous gripping with the knees has been abandoned, the inside of the knee must always lie against the saddle ready to grip if needed, just as the inside of the calf is always in the right place waiting to give aids. Then, if the rider loses his balance through a sudden stumble, swerve or shy he will grip without conscious thought, and be able to use his legs at the same moment to balance or straighten the horse.

The dangers of using the back of the leg for aids is shown even more clearly when jumping, for the rider will be confronted with the choice of using his legs *or* keeping his knees on the saddle during the approach and in the middle of big combination fences, when it is quite obvious that he must do both.

Toes pointing downwards as I have already said can be a sign of a weak and inefficient seat, but there is also a bad habit of drawing the heels upwards when giving aids which is usually acquired by riding ponies too small for you.

This raising of the heel will loosen the knee which will loosen the thigh and so in the act of applying a leg aid you will lose the driving powers of your thighs and seat. This will not have mattered

7

when careering about on small ponies, but it will be a severe disadvantage when it comes to serious schooling; you must be able to sit correctly while giving aids if you are to maintain the horse's impulsion and rhythm.

LOOKING DOWN

Your horse is profoundly influenced by your weight, and your head is heavy. If you look where you are going you will give your horse advance warning of your intentions. This is particularly important when jumping courses as the experienced horse will turn in the air and land with the correct leading leg if only you will tell him where you want to go. By looking down you lose a valuable aid. Luckily it is an easily eradicated fault, needing only determination for a cure. Give yourself points to look at in the school, take an interest in trees and clouds. Always look for the next jump even when there is none.

Rounded backs, which sometimes go with looking down, are often caused by an incorrect seat. The rider feels that he is behind the movement of the horse and tries to compensate by bringing his *shoulders* forward. Of course he should correct the situation by bringing his seatbones forward and moving his lower leg back.

Sitting slumped in the saddle is a bad habit to get into for it is very hard on the horse's back. If you feel exhausted he is probably tired too, so it would be far better to dismount and give both of you a rest.

When riding with jumping stirrups one should never sit down for the same reason. You will not be able to sit in the lowest part of the saddle, your stirrups will force you back and your weight will be too near the horse's loins. While one has jumping stirrups one always sits forward with one's weight on the thighs, knees and stirrups, not on the seatbones.

THE HAND POSITION

The hands come second to the seat because they are completely dependant on it for their skill and success. Until you have a secure seat you cannot keep your hands still, and therefore you should not attempt a contact with the horse's mouth. Once the seat is

8

established the quality of the contact you take up will depend on the correctness of the seat, but there are bad habits, faults and incorrect positions of the hands which can be acquired despite a correct seat. So, having sorted out your seat and leg position take a long hard look at your hands. Once again there is a straight line to help you. This one runs from the bit, along the reins, through the rider's hand to his elbow and any deviation from it will have a braking effect on the horse's mouth and will prevent him rounding his back and coming on the bit. The fact that he cannot round his back will prevent his hind legs coming under his body and make it impossible for him to become the better balanced, shortened, and finally collectable horse that it is our aim to produce. It will also prevent him from realizing his best action.

Though the position of the hands changes for jumping the straight line from bit to elbow still applies, but there is one fault that the rule does not detect: the too-short rein. In the jumping seat, as I have already said, the rider's shoulders move forward, he shortens his reins and his elbows leave his sides, but the reins must not be too short or the elbows will be fully extended during the approach. If this happens the rider has nothing left to give, and he becomes incapable of allowing the horse the freedom of his head and neck over the fence. The rider's seat and weight must stay over the saddle, it is the elbows' duty to extend gradually, allowing the hands to keep contact as the horse stretches out and returning to the approach position as he lands. Too short a rein makes this impossible, and the boldest horse will sicken of jumping if he is obstructed in this way.

When carrying a whip, and one should always carry a whip, especially on a horse one is schooling, it is important to make sure that it lies halfway down the thigh and points downwards. Whips carried horizontally, pointing towards the rider's hip, break our straight line by turning the whip hand downwards, which means that the contact will be too strong on one side of the horse's mouth and will cause obvious problems of unevenness of stride.

A few riders carry their hands above the level of the rein, but this is usually a beginner's fault, the more experienced rider tends to lower them for, by stiffening the elbow and setting the hands below the level of our straight line, it is possible to make the horse *look* as though he is on the bit to the extent that his nose is dropped. The expert will see that the hind legs are not coming under the body, but it is possible to fool quite a lot of people with this false headcarriage and it is also possible to win Pony Club and novice dressage tests with it. In more advanced dressage tests the more difficult movements will show up the lack of impulsion and un-engaged hind legs and the rider will find that he has to go back to the beginning and re-school the horse with a correct hand position if he is to go further. Worse still, this setting of the hands, again by preventing the rounding off the back and the use of the hind leg, will spoil the horse's jumping. Another faulty hand position, rather harder to detect, is the rounded wrist. Here again the straight line from bit to elbow is broken, not by being above or below the line but by turning the hands inwards. About forty years ago there was a great fashion for riding with rounded or bent wrists and though it was soon abandoned by dressage and jumping experts it persisted for some time in the show ring and occasionally re-appears today. If you experiment you will find that instead of a sympathetic following contact of the straight wrist and the feeling of a free elbow there is a stiffness, the hands become stationary and there is a braking action in the contact that will put the horse behind the bit instead of on it.

A few people manage to bend their hands outwards instead of inwards with the same stiffening of the wrists and the same bad effect on the horse.

All faulty hand positions defeat your purpose and make your schooling wasted time. Your end product will be a dreary horse that is behind the bit most of the time, but, if he is high-couraged, he may seize the opportunity to escape from your perpetual braking when being ridden in the open. Because you have not gained *control* of the hind legs, you have merely prevented him using them, so when excited he will become as uncontrollable as any unschooled horse.

If as well as a faulty hand position you use strong driving aids in your determination to put your horse on the bit, you will produce a frustrated, uneven striding animal, ears back, tail swishing, unable to explain that you have put him in an impossible position by demanding impulsion with your legs and seat, while you prevent him from producing it with your hands.

ERADICATING YOUR FAULTS

It is not easy to abandon bad habits and in riding major changes of leg position or seat can make one feel insecure and unhappy for a time. Obviously then all violent changes should be made before the new horse is acquired, using the old pony whose familiarity will leave one free to concentrate entirely on oneself.

Another way would be to take some lessons from a really good instructor. But instructors cannot actually cure faults, They can point them out, explain their cause and suggest ways of correcting them, but it is the rider who must do the work and cure himself.

If a study of yourself by mirror, shop window and photograph convinces you that your seat is horrifyingly incorrect, do not despair; try to arrange for yourself to be lunged by a sensible friend on a smooth, quiet horse. Lungeing is good because, relieved of the responsibility of control, you can sit in a relaxed manner, holding on to the pommel at first, and concentrate on sorting out your seat.

On the other hand you may feel that you have managed quite well in your riding career, you have won a good many rosettes despite your faults so why bother to change? The answer is that faults make difficulties for you and your horse and the greater your ambition and the further you advance the more barrier-like these difficulties will become.

It is obvious that if you cannot find or cannot afford a perfect horse, buying a suitable one is largely a matter of matching your circumstances, shape, temperament, talents and ambitions in some sensible order of priority. To do this you need a degree of self-knowledge that many riders do not possess and so, before you actually set out to buy the horse, perhaps you should take stock of yourself as a rider.

2

Finding a Suitable Horse

The perfect horse is seven years old, sound, with good conformation, natural balance and a calm but willing temperament. He is well-schooled, a good jumper and fast. He is traffic-proof, easy to catch, box, shoe and inject. He is a good doer and kind in the stable. But naturally a horse with so many virtues is extremely expensive, and most of us have to make do with less than perfection. The important thing to decide before you go horse-hunting is, which virtues are essential to you and which you are prepared to do without.

PRIORITIES

Old horses, young horses, the ugly, the bad-tempered, the unsound, the badly-schooled, the temperamental, the traffic-shy, the unsuccessful and the untalented should all be cheaper, but to avoid an expensive false economy you must consider your own particular circumstances. For the ordinary owner I would make soundness the first priority for, with the present high price of horse feed, it is obviously madness to saddle oneself with an unridable animal unless one is a farmer with plenty of keep who can afford to turn him out and wait for recovery.

My second priority would be reasonable conformation. Some people feel that conformation is only important for the show horse but this is not so, though once again the use to which the horse is to be put will have a bearing on which faults in conformation are acceptable and which are not. A strong, thick neck and a great broad chest would be virtues if one was buying a horse to pull heavy loads, but a terrible disadvantage if one wanted a fast and lively riding horse. A straight shoulder and a short stride, besides giving you that feeling of riding on the ears will, especially if combined with straight pasterns, make the horse's legs suffer far more jar. In a showjumper performing on hard-baked ground all summer, this could lead to navicular or ringbone. A horse with small, weak or sickle hocks will not stand up to jumping out of heavy going or a very hilly countryside. Nor will he be suitable to train for advanced dressage, for a collected horse carries so much of his own and his rider's weight on the hindquarters that a strong hock is needed. Horses with very long cannon bones are more susceptible to sprains than those with short ones. Horses with flat soles suffer on stony lanes and boulder-strewn moorlands. Long-backed, herring-gutted horses will be bad doers and therefore expensive to feed. Horses with ewe necks need very careful riding if they are not to become stargazers, while those with huge heavy heads will plod along on their forehands, and though they can be improved by schooling, will never be first-class rides. A badly set-on head with very little space between cheek and neck can make it difficult for the horse to drop his nose and come on the bit. This is also true of an adult horse whose quarters are higher than his withers, though his problem will be bringing his hind legs under his body. Both these faults in conformation need slow and sympathetic schooling, for the horse will fight attempts to *force* him into the correct shape to escape the discomfort involved.

Apart from the point by point appearance of the horse, the general picture is important. Your attitude to the blood, bone and frame of the horse will be influenced by your weight and by balancing your needs for staying power and speed.

Blood in horse terms means thoroughbred blood, racehorse ancestors, and so speed but not toughness. Bone means the measurement round the leg, cannon bone and tendons, immediately below the knee. Immense bone is not required in a riding horse except for heavy-weight riders, but very slender fragile-looking legs do not stand up to really hard work. As for the frame of the horse one needs a fairly wide chest and a deep girth for heart and lung room, and the well-sprung ribs that usually denote a good doer. If he is too wide-chested and too broad-backed he will be a slow and cumbersome ride, and the effort of heaving all his weight over fences will be too much for him to make a really good jumper.

The blood weed, a narrow-chested, well-bred little horse with both legs, as they say, coming out of the same hole, is not capable of great endurance or of carrying heavy weights. They are sometimes brilliant jumpers, however, and can be a good buy for light-weight riders, provided they are not aiming for competitions where a substantial weight must be carried. Two stone of lead in your weight-cloth demands quite a strong sort of horse.

But however perfect a horse looks standing still, it is how he looks moving that really matters. If one can't afford a good-looking horse one must search around for a plain one which looks good in action. Very green horses, that is young ones broken but not yet schooled, mostly drift along in an unco-ordinated manner because they have not yet adjusted to carrying a rider's weight. Adult horses who look worse on the move than they do stationary are not usually a good buy, unless there is some obvious fault in schooling which could be corrected by good riding.

ACTION

This is a matter on which your Vet can advise you, but basically a riding horse should have a low, smooth, straight stride. If he is a rough and bumpy ride and you see a lot of his knees he has the high action of a harness horse and will be slower across country than the long, low-striding horse. However, a *very* long stride can be a nuisance showjumping as the horse may find it difficult to adjust and will be unable to put in that quick short stride that is sometimes so essential.

Dishing, when the horse throws his forelegs outwards with a circular motion of the hoof, is ugly but does not really matter except in show horses; plaiting, when the horse goes very close in front, is more serious as obviously the horse can cut himself or even fall.

The perfect age, as I have said, is seven. The horse is fully grown, he will be over childish ailments like splints, any congenital defects should have emerged, and he will have had two years of experience. An older horse, say over twelve, who is sound and well should have another eight years of work ahead of him and some of them carry on much longer than this. After about sixteen very hard or fast work will become too much for him, for example hunting with a fast pack, point-to-pointing, or adult horse trials, where bonus marks across country have to be collected. But he will still be capable of hunting in a slower country once a week, of riding club and Pony Club horse trials and of show jumping and dressage tests.

The old horse is set in his ways and if he has faults and bad habits they will be very hard to change. Unless you consider them to have been directly caused by his present rider, you must be prepared to accept him as he is. If he circles with an incorrect bend you should be able to get him looking the right way but you will never get him really supple as you would a young horse. If he has developed his own distinct style of jumping you will probably have to adapt and adjust to him rather than the other way round.

On the other hand, if you have no time for schooling, if you are taken up with your own education or are at boarding school and do not possess horsey parents, the very unalterability of the older horse becomes an advantage. You will find the same horse at the beginning of every holidays. He will not have forgotten his schooling or thought up some new method of getting his own way, or dreamed up some fantasy about what lives under plastic sheeting; and he will not be thoroughly overfresh and out of hand just when you are out of practice. All you will have to do is to get him fit and then you will be able to rely on his usual performance.

So an old horse with talent can be a good buy, provided that you do not ask too much of him and that you treat him with tact and respect.

Horses and ponies under five years are, quite rightly, ineligible for Pony Club teams. They should not be given a full day's hunting or entered for any but the most novice of cross-country and dressage competitions and they should not be show-jumped.

Horses, like people, mature at different ages and racehorses are specially fed to bring them on, but it must be remembered that a racehorse is referred to as 'old' at four and is often broken-down. Since the larger proportion of them are destined to retire to stud and be used for breeding purposes only, this does not matter. A riding horse is a very different matter. We want to make use of all the schooling we have done and of all the experience the horse has gained, we want to keep him sound and workable for sixteen or seventeen years and so we must build him slowly and system-atically into the strong, powerful and well-schooled animal that we all want to possess.

A three-year-old can be lunged quietly, backed and walked about a paddock the autumn he is three-and-a-half. The best plan then is usually to turn him away for the winter—who wants to ride a green horse on frozen ground anyway? His real education should start in the spring when he is four.

A four-year-old should continue work on the lunge and do a lot of hacking, preferably with a schoolmaster—an older sensible horse—as a companion. He should be ridden up and down hills and over uneven ground to develop his muscles and improve his balance. He should be popped over a large variety of small jumps and he should gradually increase his work in the school.

Regrettably, it is usually the best four-year-olds which are spoiled: their owners, finding they have talent, rush them into competitions long before they are physically and mentally ready. If you have a promising jumper take him to the show by all means but ride him in the showing class—he may not have a chance but it will give him valuable experience and he will get over the excitement of it all before he actually has to contend with the jumping.

To be a good jumper the horse must enjoy the motion and be bursting with confidence. Show jumps are hefty, and if you crash your youngster into some difficult combination before he has the experience and strength to cope with it you can easily put him off jumping for life.

A five-year-old needs patience too and obviously you have to be very selective about the competitions for which you enter, but at least he is full grown and ready to collect experience.

Another disadvantage of owning a young horse is finding the time for all this schooling. If you are at boarding school or working hard at 'O' or 'A' levels you simply will not be able to give him the continuous, steady work he needs so, unless you have an experienced rider to help you or your parents are prepared to send the horse somewhere to be schooled do not undertake a youngster. People who have weekends and summer evenings free should be able to produce a well-schooled four-year-old between April and October.

If you do decide on a young horse choose one with reasonable conformation, a nice head, and a kind temperament. It is bitter if, at the end of a year's work and the practice of much patience, you find yourself landed with a dud or a juvenile delinquent. Be particular about size. While you do not want an enormous prancing youngster to cope with you do want something that will still fit you at the end of a couple of years, otherwise you will not reap the benefit of all your work. And there are benefits in training your own young horse. Beside the material ones of a long working life ahead and the saving on price, there is no closer partnership than with the horse one has trained oneself—and then there is your pride in him and the tremendous experience you have gained.

So a young horse can be a good buy if you have enough time, or if there is someone to help you, or if he can be sent away to be schooled. But since it is definitely cruel to work a three-year-old hard and stupidly short-sighted to be ambitious with a four-year-old, do not buy a youngster unless you have plenty of patience.

TALENTED HORSES

If you are ambitious talent is one thing you absolutely must have in your horse, but since proved talent is tremendously expensive most of us have to try to recognize it in the rough. You can school a horse to jump a clear round over the height of which he is capable. You can teach him to jump seemingly terrifying objects, to take straights and spreads, to be clever at combinations, to have impulsion and to accept the half halt, and you can build up his strength and self-confidence. But at the end of all that if he is not a talented jumper, if he has no spring or scope, or lacks a good brain and some courage, you still will not have a good jumper, just a well-schooled horse. To ask a horse to jump higher than he can is to make his life a misery of banged and bruised legs and lost self-confidence.

So decide whether your aim is riding club, Pony Club, fox-hunter, grade C or grade A, and work out the height you will need. For cross-country a bolder horse is needed but not the ability to jump high that is essential in a first class showjumper.

Dressage at the novice level does not demand much talent but if you want to train a horse on for more advanced competitions it would be madness to waste the time and effort on an untalented animal. You must have good action, natural balance, a calm temperament and 'presence' for an advanced dressage horse. Since nothing loses more marks than boiling over, all prancers, joggers and shyers are out as are irritable horses who swish their tails, grind their teeth and go with their ears back, and also neurotic mares.

So, if you only want to hack, a horse that is a pleasant ride will do. If you are content with the ordinary riding club or Pony Club competition a small talent is all that is necessary—but if you are ambitious you must find a horse with the right talents, for his sake as well as your own.

UNSUCCESSFUL HORSES

Being unsuccessful does not necessarily mean that you are without talent. It is possible to find a horse that has been hiding his light under a bushel, either because his owner rides badly or because he is not interested in the particular branch of riding where the horse's talents lie. Top horse trial horses have been found in the hunting field carrying owners who appreciated their jumping ability but had no idea just how good they were. A potential dressage horse will get nowhere if his rider has an incorrect seat.

My sisters and I once bought a pony though we were assured by the sellers that he never jumped in the ring. He had a tremendous jump, he was light and well-balanced with a huge eye and a generous expression and we decided to take a chance on the possibility that his rider was at fault. Snowman jumped three clear rounds at his first show and won prizes showjumping for many years with two different riders.

So you can buy an unsuccessful horse if your riding ability compares favourably with the seller's or if you are going to offer a fresh start in some new field of horse activity. If you are an experienced rider with plenty of time, buying the unsuccessful can be a very rewarding way of collecting horses.

SEX

In the Middle Ages no knight would ever ride a mare; they were only considered suitable for clerics, second class travellers and farm work, but it was a fashion with a sensible reason behind it. To keep up the supply of horses for transport, pleasure and war the mares had to be bred from, and since the period of gestation for foals is longer than that for humans—nearly eleven months— a mare was almost always either carrying or feeding a foal. Consequently she could only do slow steady work, and was quite unsuitable for battle.

The showiness and muscular development of the stallion, and his natural instinct to perform movements such as the passage, give him an advantage over mares and geldings as a high school horse, and the Spanish Riding School still breeds from its mares and performs on its stallions. In flat racing the colts are kept as entires and if successful will go to stud at the end of their racing career. If unsuccessful they are gelded and sold as hurdlers, steeplechasers or riding horses.

Because nowadays most people want to ride their mares and not breed from them a stallion is considered too much of a liability for the ordinary owner and so one's choice is generally limited to a mare or gelding.

Even so, one horse of each sex kept together can cause a maddeningly romantic affair with hysterical neighing at every separation, but this can also happen with two of the same sex. Kicking when turned out is usually less in a single sex field than when the sexes are mixed. But the chief reason for buying a gelding is that they are considered far more reliable for competition riding. Mares are liable to be temperamental when in season and this happens every three weeks during the summer months. On the other hand, if a mare has an accident which makes her unridable she can usually be bred from, while in the same circumstances a gelding would be useless and would probably be put down.

COLOUR

There are more rhymes and sayings about colour than about any other aspect of choosing a horse, which seems odd because apart from matching a pair of show horses or collecting a four-in-hand it is only a matter of taste, and so relatively unimportant. Probably the most sensible saying is that 'A good horse is never a bad colour.'

However, it *is* true that white socks do seem more prone to cracked heels and mud fever than black points but this could be due to the extra washing, black legs only get brushed. *Some* grey horses do get Melanosis as they grow older and whiter, and the pigment leaves the skin and collects in lumps in the tissues. Roans and duns *are* usually tough and have a pony cleverness, for they have a strain of the early Celtic pony in them which improves both the large, stupid northern horse and the brilliant, oversensitive southern horse—but that is going a long way back into evolution.

TRAFFIC-SHYNESS

If you have only to cross one road to reach miles of moorland or if you only school at home and have your own transport to take you to shows, a traffic-shy horse won't bother you and you should be able to get something knocked off his price.

But for most of us who want to enjoy hacking and who expect our mounts to transport themselves to Pony Club rallies and meets and who want to join in treasure hunts and picnic rides, the traffic-shy horse is a misery and a menace, especially when riding alone.

Young horses reared on secluded farms are sometimes nervous of traffic and this can normally be overcome by taking them out with a schoolmaster, but the really traffic-shy adult horse seems impossible to cure completely and is a risk not only to himself and his owner but to other road users as well.

The sort of horse that shys out *into* the traffic under the mis-apprehension that pieces of paper on banks, dogs yapping at their gates and manhole covers are all far more dangerous than cars, needs schooling. Once he reaches the stage of shoulder-in he will be controllable, as the rider will be able to ride forward with the head to the traffic. Young horses which play up in this way should only be taken on the road with a schoolmaster in the lead.

TEMPERAMENT

This is largely a question of suiting the two of you, for the sort of horse that drives one rider mad is cheerfully accepted by another, but since your whole partnership depends on your being in sympathy with one another it is very important. No rider should feel ashamed that he is not equally sympathetic towards all horses, but nor should he feel an urge to run down the sort that do not suit him. This is not a matter of right and wrong but merely a question of matching. So if joggers and prancers drive you into a mouth-jagging rage do not buy one, however well he jumps. And if the fast, keen horse frightens you into holding him on a perpetually tight rein leave him for someone else and find a steady sober horse which you can set alight.

Many well-bred horses are sensitive, thin-skinned and irritable, and allowance has to be made for this both in one's aids and one's grooming. If your temperament is the sort that knocks the mud off with a dandy brush and sets off with a kick and a wallop leave the well-bred horse for those with body brushes and light aids.

Bad-tempered horses, and it is often the badly handled thin-skinned sort that become bad-tempered, are very depressing to live with. To be greeted with pricked ears and a whinny is one of the pleasures of horse owning and one deprives oneself of a great deal if one buys an unfriendly horse. And if, as well as a perpetually cross face, one suffers the daily discomfort of being bitten and kicked there will not be much pleasure in the relationship.

So, unless you are exceptionally tough—bad-tempered horses become steadily worse if their owners are afraid of them—and he is exceptionally talented, leave him for someone who has a stableful of horses and will not be depressed by one scowling face. In families where there are younger brothers and sisters a bad-tempered horse can be dangerous and it is better not to run the risk of accidents, however brilliant a performer he is.

Rearers, jibbers, bolters, confirmed kickers and confirmed buckers, if they get you off, are not for the person who rides for pleasure. Leave them for experienced professionals to sort out.

UNCO-OPERATIVE HORSES

If, as well as possessing good conformation and talent, your horse is co-operative in small matters—holds up his hoofs for the blacksmith, walks into the trailer unattended, puts his head into the headcollar when you appear in the field and has a blind faith in the healing powers of vets, you are a very lucky owner, for horses that are not easy to catch, box and shoe are great time-wasters. With a young horse you have of course to teach him that being shod and travelling in trailers are perfectly safe and normal ways of spending his time. This is done by tapping his hoofs with hammers and leading him in and out of trailers, and rewarding him with praise and tit-bits until it all becomes a pleasure rather than an ordeal to him.

Whether you can cope with an adult horse that is difficult to shoe depends on whether you have a strong but kind blacksmith. Tranquilizers are sometimes effective and sensible general handling will probably cure him in the end, but unless you and your blacksmith are fairly tough it is best not to land yourself with this problem.

Adult horses that will not box have sometimes had a frightening journey so two-wheeled trailers and bad drivers should be avoided.

The fear of being caught seems to be a sign of bad handling in early life, for the horses one has bred oneself are never any trouble in this way even when disinclined for work. We had a young horse who, lying down in the field on sunny mornings, would flop over on his side and shut his eyes tightly at the sound of our voices. While you put on his headcollar, shook his hoofs, slapped his rump and tried to prise his eyes open he would go on with his pretence of being asleep, only getting up when he realized that his companions were all caught and going without him. This sort of experience with young horses has convinced me that not wishing to be caught is caused by some old half-buried experience which leaves the horse neurotic.

The cure is to catch him frequently. So turn him out in a headcollar (or with a strap round his neck if he is inclined to scratch his ears with a hind hoof) in the smallest field at your disposal and catch him not just for work but for every feed and every tit-bit and sometimes just for a pat and a talk.

STABLE VICES

Stable vices are a matter on which one should take one's Vet's advice, but since they offer a way of acquiring a talented horse cheaply you may need to know about them.

Weaving, crib-biting and wind-sucking are all neurotic habits often acquired during long periods of boredom, as when stable-bound through illness or lameness, but they can also be learned from watching a horse with the habit. A mare may teach her foal to crib-bite; a whole yardful of horses may copy one weaver.

Weaving is the least detrimental to health, though a horse

23

perpetually swinging his weight from one pair of lateral legs to the other obviously does not rest as well as a normal horse and a whole yardful of weavers, their heads swaying from side to side as they look out over their stable doors, is enough to drive the sanest owner mad.

In crib-biting the horse seizes hold of something solid with his teeth—the manger, the top of the door, a fence-post in the field—and sucks air into his stomach. This habit is definitely bad for a horse's digestion and makes it difficult to get and keep him fit. He will usually look thin along his back but carry a large belly below. His teeth may also become worn down.

Wind-sucking is usually resorted to when crib-biting has been prevented by removing all edges and ledges or covering them with a disgusting substance. The horse stands in the middle of his box, arches his neck and gulps down air. This can be discouraged by a strap round the top of the neck with a disc which fits into the gullet and causes discomfort if the neck is arched.

Since stable vices create problems of fitness and of sharing stables and fields with normal horses, they should be avoided unless they offer the chance of acquiring a horse of exceptional talents cheaply.

3

Trying and Buying

Having decided to buy a horse, and having got family permission and money, it is easy to be overcome with a fever of impatience and acquire some unsuitable animal on impulse. He may be golden chestnut and have a star, but if he is an enormously broad cob and you are a thin girl he is not going to be the right horse for you. So self-control is necessary and one way of dealing with your impatience is to devote the time to riding as many strange horses as possible. This is especially important if you are moving from a smallish pony on to a horse, for, if you are not used to the feel of a long neck in front of you and a long stride underneath you, you will be in no state to judge whether you like a particular horse. So bribe your friends to let you ride their larger animals or book a few lessons at a good riding school, explaining your need. At the same time practise judging all the strange horses you can; make up your mind whether they have good shoulders or bad hocks, whether they are herring-gutted or well ribbed-up. Try to form an opinion about their action, their balance and schooling, their potential. It is only by looking at and riding a great many different horses that one develops judgement.

For the same reason it is a good plan to go and see and try the first batch of horses one hears of even if they do not sound exactly what you want. You will get your eye in and gain some experience of dealing with sellers.

LOOKING AROUND
Having made up your mind what qualities are essential to you, how much you can afford to pay and what your top and bottom

age and size limits are, you have to set about finding the horse. If you belong to the Pony Club let the secretary and the district commissioner and all the instructors and members know the sort of horse you want, for buying a horse whose history is known is a great deal safer than shopping in the open market.

Buy *Horse and Hound* each week and study the advertisements but, unless you drive or your parents are really keen horse-hunters, you may find some of them too far away to see. Of course tempting-sounding advertisements of perfect horses can be misleading, so one should never be too cast down by not being able to get to distant parts of the country. The local or county paper is another place to look and these horses will all be within seeing distance.

Enquire about the horse dealers in your district, from the Pony Club or riding club secretaries if you have not many horsey contacts. Telephone all the horse dealers of which you hear good reports and tell them the sort of horse you want and the price you can pay; do not get involved with the ones you are advised against.

Nowadays there are plenty of nice, honest horse dealers and often they have been Pony Club members or showjumping enthusiasts themselves and so know exactly what you are looking for, and it is often safer to buy from them than from the private owner who may just want to pass on a horse he cannot cope with or one that is unsound. A local horse dealer knows that his successful customers are his best advertisement.

If you have decided on an older horse probably the riding and Pony Club contacts will be your most hopeful area of search; for most people like to place their old friend in a home they know something about.

If you have settled to have a young horse, a dealer who brings them over from Ireland and spends a couple of months getting them fit and schooling them on gently would be the person to find. Irish horses are usually sensible and tough, but those which have only just arrived frequently have, or are incubating, Strangles. They seem to have a lot of resistance to this disease but what with them appears to be just a slight cough and a runny nose can infect a stableful of English horses with severe Strangles. My sisters and I bought two Irish horses once and someone forgot that they were supposed to be isolated—with the result that we found ourselves taking twenty-seven temperatures night and morning as horse after horse succumbed. The worst of Strangles is that after a severe case the convalescence is lengthy, and if you ride a horse too soon you are very likely to do permanent damage to his lungs and wind.

If you can afford a brilliant seven-year-old just approaching his peak performance in competitions, you can advertise for one in *Horse and Hound*, but contacts in the appropriate field, showing, showjumping or eventing, will probably be the best way of finding him.

ELIMINATING DUDS

If you wish to save yourself a long journey it is often worth having a talk with the seller on the telephone. Obviously no one is going to run down their own horse, but a lot of sellers will avoid dragging you miles and wasting their own time if their horse is clearly unsuitable for some reason. So explain what you want, laying stress on the essential points. For instance, 'I live on a busy road so I need something that is absolutely traffic-proof. I have to ride along it for a mile to get anywhere and there are double-decker buses as well as lorries', will usually elicit a helpful answer. 'Yes, he's one hundred per cent.' Or, 'Well, he's all right in normal traffic but I'm not going to say that he wouldn't look at a double-decker bus . . .'

You can treat ability in the same way. Explain exactly what grade of showjumping or class of horse trials you propose to compete in and ask if he's up to it. Most sellers will admit that their horse is not exactly what you want if you obviously know your own mind and needs.

Horses are not as expensive to buy as houses but buying needs just as much thought and care to make sure you pick the right one, and on the open market the risk of being 'done' is about the same as when buying a second-hand car. If you and your family are inexperienced, take a knowledgeable adviser or arrange for one to see the horse of your choice before you actually write the cheque. No adviser is infallible, and anyway the final choice must be yours, but they can stop you making some mistakes. I remember when I was very young my parents took me to try a pony called Billy. He belonged to a back-street horse coper who apologised for not having a saddle, but the only one which fitted was out on the other pony. So I was legged up and led about bare-back and Billy seemed quiet enough. Of course I said he was lovely and ponies were cheaper in those days and unhorsey parents just as rash, so they bought Billy. When we got him home it turned out that he was cold-backed, or at any rate had a profound dislike of saddles, and gave the most enormous bucks when wearing them.

The moral of this story is to be suspicious of any oddity or embargo and, however convincing the reason given sounds, ask if you can come back and try him again when the saddle, bridle, field or whatever it is, becomes available. You should also take an interest in the horse's history and make a mental note of gaps when he was not ridden; they could be due to lameness or illness and should be mentioned to your vet.

Another point to check on is the reason for selling. Is he genuinely outgrown? Is his rider going to university, getting married, starting a job? Or has she just become more ambitious and is acquiring a more accomplished animal and, if so, will this one be accomplished enough for you? If no good reason for selling appears watch out for drawbacks.

MEETING A PROSPECTIVE HORSE
As you enter the stable watch your prospective horse to see how he greets his owner. Whether his ears flash back in dislike or his eyes roll nervously or whether he is calm and affectionate. Look around for signs of stable vices; crib biting, windsucking weaving. Then look at his coat and saddle mark to see if there are any signs that he has already been exercised that day. A cold-

backed horse, a wild youngster, a bucker can be quite sensible if he has had a two hour hack or even half an hour on the lunge, so any sign of sweating or of a newly sponged-out saddle mark should make you suspicious. Look at his legs for ominous swellings. Pat him and pick up front and hind hoofs.

Ask to see him ridden

His general condition is important as you will have to bear it in mind when you assess his suitability. If he's fat and unfit he will obviously be slower and quieter than when you have him hard and corn fed. If he's thin and unfit the difference is likely to be even greater, and the weak spindly three-year-old will turn into a bouncing four-year-old in a year. On the other hand the clipped cornfed horse is going to be quite a lot quieter when turned out at grass. All horses are lazy in hot weather, livelier in cold weather and behave their worst in winds.

As you watch the horse being saddled do your best to judge his conformation; remembering the points which are of especial importance to you.

SEEING HIM RIDDEN

If you ask to see the horse ridden by the seller first, before you try him, you will learn a great deal more than if you make a bee-line for the saddle yourself. Besides getting a general picture of the horse and making up your mind on the all-important point of whether he looks 'good', (co-ordinated, balanced, in harmony) when moving, you will also see the sort of rider and the sort of aids and bit he is used to. Obviously the seller will be out to display his best points so make a mental note of movements not demonstrated and try them yourself. The other advantage of going second is that should the horse turn out to rear, buck, or be uncontrollable you can say firmly that he's far too lively for you and leave. A buck may be light-hearted and caused by over freshness, but rearing can be the sign of an ungenerous nature. A horse that will jib and then threaten to rear in order to frighten his rider into giving him his own way is about the nastiest ride there is, and doing battle with a rearer is dangerous as it is easy to bring them over backwards with the rider underneath. If you see the seller trying to cover up incipient jibbing and getting the horse along by tactfully giving way, do not even bother to try it.

TRYING HIM YOURSELF

When your turn comes do not hurry, do everything slowly and deliberately. Do not allow the horse to be held in an iron grasp while you are legged up; if there is any problem about mounting you want to know if you can cope with it, so even if the horse looks unusually high, let down the stirrups or find a mounting block, but make sure that you can mount him on your own. Then put your stirrups right and move off very gently with the intention of finding out what *he* is like. The very bossy rider who leaps on and bustles the horse into this movement and that with the desire to show off his own riding learns very little about the horse. It is worth pretending to be a slightly worse rider than you are; give him the chance to buck as you break into a canter, to nap as you pass the stable or gate. Then gradually pick up the reins and put him on the bit. Discover what aids he knows. Ride round a school-sized area and on circles to see how well-balanced he is, and right round the field to see if he remains under control. Try him on both reins at the walk, trot and canter and then, if you like him, pull up your stirrups and give him a gallop. Notice if he is willing and well-balanced and fast enough for your purpose, or whether he is stiff and lumbering, or a crazy tearaway whom you stop with difficulty and then spend the next ten minutes trying to calm down.

Next tell the seller that you would like to try the horse over a jump, and insist on starting low. It is never fair on a horse to jump large fences before you are used to each other. Having got your small jumps don't ride at them as though your life depended on it, you will learn far more about the horse if you let him carry you over. As they are his own familiar fences he is hardly likely to refuse them, but you will get some idea of his spring and scope and of his enthusiasm for jumping. You want pricked ears and interest but not wild excitement.

When you are used to him try something higher, and then attempt to work out some sort of course or combination so that you can judge how balanced and controllable he remains between the fences; whether he loses his impulsion, and whether he is clever at adjusting his stride.

If you are buying a schooled horse, say a Grade C jumper, you will expect to try him over a four-foot course and a schooled cross-country horse should be tried over natural fences with ditches and water unless his reputation is too great to warrant this. But if you are trying a young horse the odd jump of three foot three should be the limit of your demands.

If being quiet in traffic is important ask if you can try him on the roads. Some sellers are quite willing to take a prospective buyer for a hack which is a very good way to get to know a strange horse.

It is quite usual to allow small, quiet ponies, suitable for beginners to go on trial and riding schools will sometimes hire out a pony for a week or two if you are interested in buying him. But the higher up the scale of value you go the less likely you are to be allowed a horse on trial. It is easy to understand the seller's point of view. A valuable horse can so easily be kicked or caught in wire leaving him lame or blemished. A well-schooled horse can be wrecked by a week of bad riding, a first-class jumper soured for life by an incompetent rider. It is too much to ask of anyone that they will hand over their valuable, well-trained horse to a stranger for a week on the off chance that he might buy him.

Some horse dealers will agree to change the horse for another if he doesn't suit. Naturally the next horse will be slightly more expensive to cover the dealer's trouble, but when someone earns their living by buying and selling horses you must expect to pay for the service.

ENSURING ELIGIBILITY

You must avoid later disappointment by checking that your horse is eligible for the classes you wish to ride in. If you are interested in Juvenile jumping, showing classes for ponies, hacks or small working hunters height may be important to you. Ask if the horse possesses a life measurement certificate and remember that young horses still growing are only issued with yearly certificates until the age of six. Horses which grow late can have their life certificates invalidated if someone objects and they are then officially re-measured and found to have grown. So, if height is really an essential point make quite sure about it, have him measured by the official Vet if necessary.

Pony Club events usually worry less about height and more about grades. If you want to be in your Pony Club inter-branch showjumping team, for instance, you must only buy a Grade A showjumper that *is* eligible for Popular Open Jumping competitions. For the Inter-branch Horse Trials a horse must not have been Grade I 'Advanced' in the British Horse Society's Combined Training Register for the last three years. Nor must he have been placed first or second in an Intermediate or Advanced horse trial during the last two years. So you must read the latest rules for the particular competitions you plan to ride in and then check that the horse is eligible.

Showjumpers are registered with the British Showjumping

Association which keeps a list of their winnings, as the B.H.S. does of the Horse Trial horses, so it is very easy to check up on the accomplished horse. You will, of course, have to notify the societies that you are the new owner. It is also essential to enquire about winnings on a much more lowly scale for sooner or later you will want to enter in a class for horses that have not won five pounds, or a class for horses that have never won a jumping competition, so you must know just how novice your horse is. If you enter recklessly you may find that someone who knows more about your horse's history than you do objects, and no one wants the embarrassment of being disqualified or to be the centre of bad feeling.

The breed societies also have registers, and so if you buy say an Anglo-Arab or Connemara you should re-register the horse in your name. If you don't intend to show this doesn't matter with geldings, but with a mare it will save a lot of bother if you want to breed from her later.

REACHING A DECISION

Now, having consulted with your adviser, who agrees that the horse, though not perfect, is a good buy, you have to make up your mind. And it must be your decision, for it is you who has to live with him for the next few years, so at the end of all the careful weighing up the crucial question is, 'Do you really like him?' If you do, just take one more look to make sure that the fact that he's a golden chestnut with a star has not blinded you to the fact that he's far too small or too broad for you, or that he's far too well-bred to live out in your windswept field. Then tell the seller that you would like to buy him, subject to your Vet's approval.

If you decide against him give your decision as tactfully as you can for sellers are often sensitive. 'He's lovely but a bit too small/excitable/green for what I want,' is a more polite way of saying bluntly that he's stunted, hysterical or badly schooled. If you cannot make up your mind say that you have one or two more horses to see and you will telephone.

You may be offered a vet's Certificate with a horse but this is not at all the same thing as sending your Vet to vet him. Of course no Vet will sign a certificate if the horse isn't sound, but the seller's Vet does not have to point out defects that may lead to trouble. Your Vet is on your side. You should tell him what you want the horse for and mention any points you are doubtful about: age, action, condition, height, stable vices, and ask for his opinion.

In the old days gipsies and disreputable horse dealers had a way of selling lame horses; they would wedge a painfully placed stone in the opposite foot to the lame one and the horse, now lame on both legs, would go more or less level. Now we have the drug *Butazoladine* which enables many chronically lame and old stiff horses to remain happily at work. Provided they receive their daily dose they are sound, so an unsuspecting buyer can pay a large sum for what he thinks is a sound horse only to find three days later when the drug wears off, that his new animal is chronic- ally and incurably lame. Here again, your Vet may be able to help you but it does look as though horse buyers of the future ought to be protected by a certificate provided by the seller stating what drugs, if any, the horse is taking.

Caveat Emptor or 'Buyer Beware' is the attitude of the law to the buying and selling of horses. There is no consumers' protection society to run to. I suppose the Trades Descriptions Act could be invoked in a few cases, but in most the descriptions would be too vague. *A Good Jumper* might jump well for one rider and badly for another. A horse that has *Hundreds of Prizes* to prove his jumping ability can be overfaced or soured and start refusing all in the matter of a week or ten days.

The answer is that if you are inexperienced buy a horse you know, or one that has been recommended to you or through a dealer who has been recommended, and if you venture out onto the open market take an adviser and use your own Vet.

BRINGING THE NEW HORSE HOME

Do not expose the new horse to the criticism of your friends. Do not let them all try him. You know he cannot please everyone;

he is meant to suit *you* and now you have bought him you want to be left alone to get used to each other.

Take him hacking, give him several days to settle down before you start trying to find out how high he can jump and, above all, do not enter him for a competition which demands a partnership between horse and rider until you have formed one.

4

Elementary Schooling

Successful schooling is largely a matter of the rider's attitude to his horse. It is true that you have to work hard, and that the more knowledgeable you are the further you will be able to go, but it is possible to school energetically for hours and to be bursting with knowledge and yet produce only unhappy results if you are not prepared to study and understand and adapt to the horse.

The more authoritarian rider sometimes forgets that the schooled horse must be supple as well as obedient and to be supple he must be relaxed. To learn to relax he must be calm and a horse cannot be calm unless his rider is relaxed and calm. Too many riders come to the conclusion that the horse which does not do as they want is being obstinate or stupid instead of looking on the difficulty as a misunderstanding which could be solved by a clearer explanation, by more carefully applied aids, by making the movement easier, the circle larger, the jump smaller, the position less demanding.

It is essential to study each horse as an individual. To find out his strengths and weaknesses, to consider his character and intelligence and then work out your programme and methods to suit him. The stupid horse will need simple explanations, and a lot of repetition, which means slower progress, but he is generally co-operative. The idle horse will need short bursts of energetic riding, a lot of variation to keep him alert, the company of other horses to make him more competitive—but he is generally calm and relaxed so you start with that advantage.

The clever horse must be kept calm and happy; he must enjoy his work, for as long as he is on your side things go well, but make an enemy of him and he will use his brain to outwit you and can turn into a real rogue.

The well-bred horse is often sensitive and high-couraged and this makes him fight you rather than submit to discomfort or bullying. This means that you must use tact when teaching him exercises that are difficult for him and therefore produce aching muscles. If he fails to understand your aids for a new movement and offers all the others you have taught him, you must explain that they are not what you want gently and try again; punishing him with rough aids will hurt, confuse and anger a well-bred horse.

Though the aim of schooling is to build up a partnership with the horse, the trainer begins in the position of a very senior partner. As they learn clever horses will often improve on what they have been taught, but in the beginning the trainer must initiate everything and his first aim is to establish a system of communication.

THE AIDS

The aids are the signals by which the rider communicates his wishes to the horse. They are not instinctive; the horse is not born knowing them, nor does his mother tell him; every horse has to be taught them by the person who breaks and schools him.

The aids do not compel; there is no reason to obey them: only good-nature and habit. The unspoiled horse is an affable and willing creature and is usually happy to oblige if he is fit enough, balanced and supple enough, if he is not too excited to think and he understands what his rider means.

In some old books on horsemanship the aids are called 'the helpes' which is rather a nice way of putting it. They should help the rider to explain politely and pleasantly what he would like his horse to do; they should be as light and as nearly invisible as is possible, and they should never degenerate into kicking and pulling.

It would, of course, be perfectly easy to teach a young horse to obey secret aids known only to him and his trainer, but this would make life very difficult for him if he was ridden by anyone else. It is possible to use music as an aid, changing the tune for a change of pace as is done in circuses, but it would be rather inconvenient for the riders to carry their music about with them, and with everyone playing different tunes a ringful of horses would be thrown into total confusion.

No, obviously the best aids are silent, personal, but universally known and used. They must have split-second application for jumping at speed and yet be capable of obtaining a very slow halt from the walk. They must build up logically from the simple to the complex so that what the green youngster learns is the basis of the aids for the most complicated of dressage movements.

THE VOICE

Though a fully schooled horse should obey silent aids the first aid a young horse learns is the voice. A well-brought up foal learns 'Whoa' and 'Walk on' as he is led from stable to field with his mother. Later, on the lunge, he learns 'Trot' and 'Canter', he learns 'Come here' and what the clicking of the tongue means—and another very important lesson, not to fear the whip but always to move forward away from it.

Words of command must always be given clearly and not lost in a spate of other words and the trainer must be careful how he says them. Walk, trot and canter are all called out briskly when the horse is intended to move into a faster pace but when used to indicate a slower pace they are said slowly and in a drawn-out manner; they become 'tr-ot' and 'wa-lk'. In fact the way words are said is often more important to the horse than the words themselves; he certainly will not recognise 'Whoa' if it is screamed in terror or 'Steady' repeated in a nervous gabble. There was an instance of this sort of confusion once at a gymkhana. The starter was rather enjoying his position of authority and exercising the strictest control. He grew angrier and angrier as the ponies shot into a gallop at every cry of 'Ready, steady, No!' But to the ponies his yell of No! was indistinguishable from Go! and they were completely mystified at being endlessly brought back and restarted.

THE TRANSITION TO REIN AND LEG AIDS

When a horse has been backed, that is ridden for the first time, and carries a rider with confidence, he has to be taught to associate the rein and leg aids with the words he already knows. This is done with an assistant leading him on the lunge. The rider says 'Walk on' and applies the legs, and the assistant marches forward. To halt the rider applies the aids, says 'Whoa', and the assistant halts. In this way correct, light aids can be used from the start, there is no attempt to force anything and the horse remains happy. Gradually, over two or three lessons, the assistant becomes slower and slower at obeying the commands. He lengthens the lunge rein and drops back, following the horse as he obeys the rider's aids, but ready to help if needed.

Turning is taught in the same way and, though there are no words of command to help, the horse now realizes that reins and legs give signals. At first the rider has to give a rather obvious rein-aid but he does this by moving his hand sideways, never backwards which would cause the horse to lose impulsion. Just before giving the aids the rider will tell his assistant that he is going to turn right or left. The assistant will turn and the horse will follow. Then gradually the leader will drop back, he will make his turn later and later until the horse is taking his orders entirely from the rider.

Once the horse has learned the meaning of the simple aids he can be ridden loose. But, since the aids do not compel, he must be kept very quiet and calm until obedience to them has become a habit. If he becomes too excited or too unbalanced to obey an aid he is going to learn that they can be disobeyed, and if the rider then resorts to force, the horse will have to find a way of escape from the pain of a roughly used bit. All the problems of a bad mouth, stargazing, pulling, putting the tongue over the bit, will begin. Once a horse has been schooled, once he is balanced, supple and has a steady head-carriage, once he has developed the muscles which make it easy for him to go correctly, it will be quite difficult to spoil him permanently. But at this stage one hunt, one wild ride, one afternoon's races with friends, can do an unbelievable amount of damage, the sort of damage that will take an experienced horseman months to put right.

The whip The good rider is not content with avoiding rough aids.

He tries to make his everyday aids lighter and lighter, and this applies to leg as well as rein aids. He rides his horse forward at every stride but this is not obvious for he has taught the horse to obey a light pressure of the calves.

With a thin-skinned sensitive horse this is not difficult, but with a sluggish animal there is a temptation to kick and the owner who gives way to this condemns himself to a life-time of kicking. The answer is a long schooling whip, which can be used without taking the hand from the rein, and a sharp tap is administered just behind the rider's leg every time an aid is ignored. Even on a lively horse some sort of whip should always be carried to enforce an ignored aid, and the rider should change the whip hand at intervals until he is equally at home with it in either hand.

Shouting Shouting and swearing at horses count as rough aids and sound horrible. Like all rough aids, shouting should be kept for emergencies and can then be very effective in say stopping two horses who are about to kick. Constant cries of Hup! and Grhh! and Ssssh! at horses about to jump sound amateurish and are not nearly as effective as correctly-used legs. The properly brought-up know that you must never be rude to someone who cannot answer back and that includes the horse.

HACKING

At this stage in his education the horse should leave the school and be ridden in the open. Hacking with a schoolmaster, an older, more sensible horse, will teach him that being ridden is enjoyable. He will see the world and learn not to be afraid of garden gates and manhole covers and sitting dogs and going between two walls. He will build up muscles, adapt to carrying the weight of a rider and, most important of all, he will learn to go forward freely. In the walk he should go on a long rein giving the rider the feeling that two thirds of his horse are in front of him and only one third behind. At this stage the horse should be long and low and any attempt to force him into the compact shape of the schooled horse would be quite wrong and would drive him behind the bit. The rider should forget the head-carriage and concentrate on the hind legs, for when they have become strong and active the rest will follow.

The trot should be a rising one, for the young horse's back is not yet strong enough to take a sitting rider, and there should be no attempt to canter, but a gallop is quite in order, provided there is plenty of room to stop and start the unwieldy youngster without resorting to rough aids.

For the first gallop it is best to choose an uphill field or one that ends with a rise as this will discourage bucking and make stopping easy. The schoolmaster goes ahead if his pupil is idle or apprehensive and behind if he is excitable or inclined to race. The rider must keep his hands steady and let the young horse lean on them, he will be very long and low and on the forehand, but as long as he is going forward freely that is all that matters at this stage.

As the horse becomes stronger the rider will look for uneven ground, for hills to ride up and down, for little quarries and then for logs and small ditches which he can pop over from the walk and trot. With the help of the schoolmaster the young horse becomes bold, the rider does not have to use force, going across unknown country becomes a pleasure and not an ordeal and when the young horse is obviously confident, or even over-confident, he can take the lead.

THE SCHOOL

As the young horse grows stronger, as he tires less quickly and begins to carry the rider's weight with ease, we can begin work in the school. Fifteen minutes is enough at first and this can be gradually increased to thirty minutes and followed by a short hack. Forty-five minutes to an hour of concentrated schooling is enough for any horse and for most riders.

When in a group school work is inclined to be less concentrated as there is a certain amount of standing about and waiting for the instructor's attention.

The school itself is a very useful piece of equipment. It should be roughly twenty metres by forty metres (twenty-two yards by forty-four yards) the size of a dressage arena, for working one

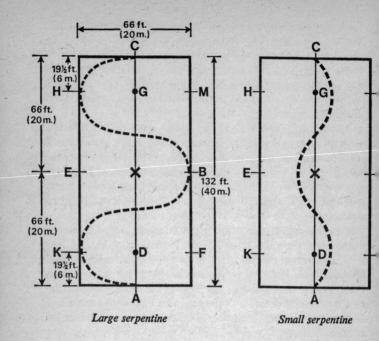

Large serpentine

Small serpentine

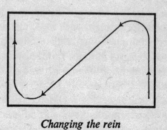

Changing the rein

horse at a time; larger if several horses are to be worked together. It should be marked out with posts or large stones at the corners, and half and quarter markers too, if possible. Drifting vaguely round an unmarked area is too easy and does not expose problems and weaknesses as riding in the marked school does.

When teaching riding it is usual to make beginners ride outside the four corner markers until they have learned to steer, but afterwards it is correct to ride inside, for a corner should always be ridden as a segment of a circle and never as a right-angle.

Though riding up and down hill has done a lot to strengthen the horse's hind legs the constant cornering which riding round a school entails will do infinitely more. And, provided the horse is not hindered or obstructed by faults in the rider's seat or hands, work in the school will, of itself, change his shape from the long, low form of the youngster into the shorter, more upright form of the schooled horse.

Obviously in the small space of the school the rider cannot ride freely forward as he did across country and the time has come to take up a contact with the horse's mouth. It is at this point that many riders go wrong and it is extremely difficult to explain the feel of a correct contact, but it has to be got right. If there is no contact the horse can never come on the bit and if the contact is too strong it will prevent the horse using his hind legs energetically, and so, though he may drop his nose, he will not be truly on the bit.

To get the correct feel the rider should experiment, first by riding with no contact and then with a slightly too strong one. This can be done by fixing the hands into one of the faulty positions which break the straight line from the bit along the rein, through the rider's hand to his elbow. He will find that there is a stationary feel about the strong contact and it is this which has a braking effect and prevents the horse using his hind legs. With the correct contact the rider feels the horse's mouth but his hands go forward with it. There is no backward feeling and no stationary feeling, unless the rider is asking the horse to slow down or to halt.

Having taken up a contact the rider uses his legs and seat to put the horse on the bit, and again it is important to have the right picture in the mind's eye. The young horse going on the bit does not shorten or become collected, his nose does not move nearer his chest, in fact at the moment of going on the bit he will *lengthen* his neck, the rider will see the ears move a little further away from him.

The young horse must not be expected to come on the bit immediately or to stay on it for any length of time. The over-conscientious and the over-ambitious riders who nag and fiddle and fix their hands in an attempt to hurry the horse into the correct head-carriage will only spoil him; the proper attitude is to take up a contact, ride forward every stride and let the school figures and movements effect the transformation of the horse.

SCHOOL PACES

Though the walk is the pace at which the young horse is chiefly ridden out hacking the trot is the one most used in the school for, being in two-time, with the legs moving in diagonal pairs, it is the easiest pace at which to maintain impulsion while we are teaching the horse to go on the bit.

The trot can be ridden either rising or sitting. When sitting the rider obviously has a greater ability to use his seat and back to influence the horse, provided he has a good seat and can sit deep and relaxed with quiet hands. Riders who bump about, become stiff and miserable, or can only keep still by gripping, which prevents them sitting deep, are incapable of schooling the horse at the sitting trot, and must use the rising one until they have improved their seats. Young horses and horses with weak backs, usually shown by carrying their heads too high, should be schooled at the rising trot until they have developed stronger muscles.

The walk In the walk, a pace of four-time, each leg moving in turn, the horse needs much more freedom of the neck than in the trot and consequently it is even more difficult to establish a con-tact light enough not to destroy impulsion and drive him behind the bit. For this reason, in the schooling of the young horse, the walk is only used to introduce him to new movements and as a pace of rest. After an energetic period of trotting on the bit the

44

rider will give his horse a few minutes walk on a loose rein and it is a sign that his schooling is progressing satisfactorily if he will stretch out his neck and take up the loose rein.

But even when walking for a rest the horse must be ridden forward and the rider will not use both his legs together as he does at other paces, he will use them in turn. His right leg in time with the horse's right hind leg, his left with the horse's left. This is easy to do for the movement is slow and the pronounced swing of the horse's back makes it obvious what is going on beneath one.

The rider who uses his legs too quickly at the walk will cause his horse to take short, hurried steps instead of long slow ones. The horse which jogs must be calmed down and then offered a long rein in the hope that he will stretch out his neck and relax and, irritating though this habit is, the rider must remember that any display of anger on his part will only make the horse more tense and even less capable of walking.

The idle horse must be ridden forward until he overtracks, that is his hind hoof steps beyond the print left by his fore hoof on the same side. If the hind hoof print falls on top of the fore print he is not striding out as well as he can and the rider's legs should be reinforced with the long schooling whip, which is much more effective than kicking or niggling with the heels.

The canter Though the canter is an excellent pace at which to school the well-trained horse it is the most hazardous pace of all for a young one. The very unbalanced youngster will give his rider such a rough ride that any attempt to canter him round the school will probably be abandoned until his training has reached a more advanced stage. It is the naturally well-balanced and amenable young horse who is most at risk. He can get round the corners and he can obey his proud rider who slows him down into what he thinks is a collected canter. Slowed down from the front by the reins the young horse has to go behind the bit and sometimes he does this to the point where his canter becomes a pace of four-time instead of the correct three-time.

The other spoiled canter one sees quite often is the stiff-backed head-in-air polo pony canter. The horse learns to go like this from a strong rider who sticks his legs forward and uses the reins, reinforced by martingales, complicated nosebands or severe bits, to control him. Besides making the horse useless for dressage this kind of canter will make him extremely difficult to jump for, with a stiff back, the aids cannot go through and so the rider cannot shorten or extend the stride at will and the horse cannot lower his head. He will end as stiff laterally as he is from head to tail and none of his paces will be able to develop to their full potential.

So it is best to postpone cantering round the school until the horse is going on the bit and using his hind legs powerfully at the trot, this means circling, shoulder-in and the half-halt are taught first. However, cantering briskly round a large field is a different matter and out hacking a brisk and balanced canter should begin to develop from the four-year-old's rather lumbering gallop; the rider will find himself starting through a canter and slowing up through a canter and something like this, *offered* by the horse, is immensely superior to anything forced upon him.

SCHOOL FIGURES

The lively, excitable or apprehensive horse who is liable to change the length of his stride or his speed when disturbed must be ridden smoothly and calmly with only occasional changes of direction and pace for he must be encouraged to settle into a smooth rhythm. But the idle horse who plods round on his forehand, should change direction and pace frequently as this will keep him alert as well as encouraging him to use his hind legs more energetically and so take some of the weight off his forehand.

The school figures are designed to provide turns which the horse can make without shortening his stride or losing his rhythm by being thrown off balance. A good rider never makes a turn which would unbalance his horse and, except for the turn on the forehand, never turns until he is moving.

Until he has learned the pirouette the only turn a horse can make correctly is a circular one. The change of rein, for instance, is made from quarter marker to quarter marker always coming to the quarter markers from the short ride of the school. If the rider tried to change on coming to the quarter marker from the long side he would be asking for a triangular instead of a circular turn and the horse is physically incapable of this unless he can pirouette, or has learned the polo pony's version of the pirouette.

Corners The really important point about riding corners is that the horse must be bent inwards. He must look inwards, the rider must see his inside eye.

The aids are of course to feel the inside rein, use the inside leg on the girth, the outside leg slightly further back. The outside hand has a rather more complicated role: it has to permit the horse to obey the inside hand and bend his neck inwards, while at the same time maintaining contact.

On a naturally supple horse cornering is quite easy; it is on the stiff horse that the inexperienced trainer gets into trouble. For the stiff horse cannot bend, he cuts across the corner, and the rider is tempted to hold him out by using the outside rein. This is fatal for the horse is now prevented from bending and so has no hope of becoming more supple.

The answer, as usual, is to ask less and to make doing what you ask as easy as possible for the horse; to sympathise with his difficulties while being determined to overcome the problem. The corners should be ridden wide, the circles should be made enormous, only the slightest bend must be asked for, but that slight bend must be insisted upon. The rider insists with the inside aids, particularly the inside leg, and praises the smallest improvements.

A correct bend is one of those basic essentials that make or mar a horse's performance throughout his life and, since it is an outward sign of suppleness, the lack of ability to bend has far greater effects than landing one with miserably low marks in a dressage test. There are those precious seconds lost when jumping off against the clock, the propensity of a stiff horse to fall when cutting corners on slippery ground in the ring and out hunting; the lack of control should the horse decide to nap or play up in any other way.

Most of the exercises and movements used in schooling are designed to supple the horse, either from head to tail or laterally. If one moves slowly but steadily through the curriculum the horse

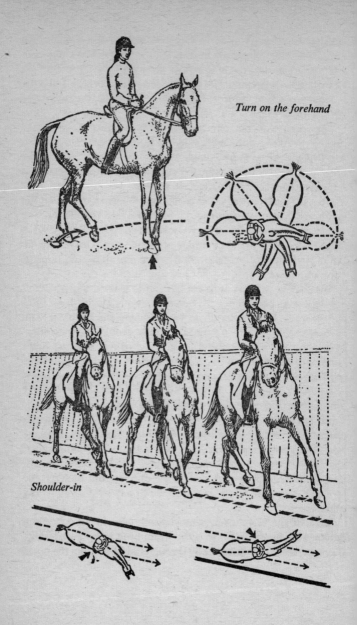

Turn on the forehand

Shoulder-in

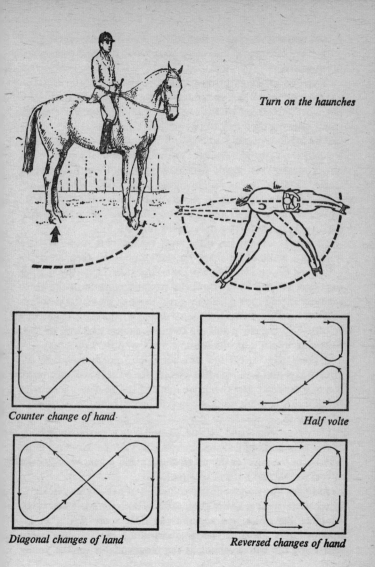

Turn on the haunches

Counter change of hand

Half volte

Diagonal changes of hand

Reversed changes of hand

should become supple however stiff he began, as long as the rider refuses to be panicked into using the outside rein and making the horse worse.

Ordinary lungeing does not make the stiff horse supple; lungeing with side-reins can, in the hands of a few great experts, help; but when attempted by the less expert results in a horse which bends only his neck and stops using his hind legs.

Circles Small circles are difficult for the horse, because his inside legs have to carry more weight while his outside legs must take a longer stride. One begins with large ones, not less than twenty metres in diameter or occupying half the school. The aids are basically those for turning. A very light feel on the inside rein, while the outside hand gives to permit the bend; the outside leg a little back, the inside leg doing most of the work.

To circle correctly the rider must visualize his route. He can imagine a white chalk mark on the ground and then bend the horse just enough to follow it; the larger the circle the slighter the bend. Having worked out the size and position of the circle the rider should look a little inwards, towards the centre point, as this will help him to keep the same distance from it the whole way round. Also the slight turning of his shoulders and hips as they follow his eyes will position him correctly on the bent horse.

A good exercise for the stiff horse is to practise making the circle larger and smaller while keeping the correct bend. To make it larger the rider uses the inside rein and leg, he *never, never* tries to enlarge it with his outside hand; to make it smaller he uses the outside aids.

Once the correct bend is achieved, and it must be the whole body that is bent and not just the horse's neck, the rider can take more interest in the pace. It should be smooth and balanced with even strides; unhurried but full of impulsion.

Serpentines The serpentine is a collection of half-circles ridden on alternate reins. It is a very good exercise both for horse and rider, suppling the horse and making the rider more skilful in his application of the aids. The large serpentine, making three loops and using the whole school, is the most suitable for the young horse as there is plenty of room to straighten him and then assume the next bend. A highly schooled horse can change almost directly from one bend to the next, a well-schooled horse needs one stride to straighten and a young horse needs several strides on the straight.

Changes of the diagonal The diagonal pairs of legs in the trot are named right and left diagonal after their forelegs. Thus the near fore and off hind are the Left Diagonal and the off fore and near hind are the Right Diagonal. The rider rises on one pair and sits on the other, but he *must* change over at regular intervals. Out hacking a good rider rises to each diagonal in turn, just as he canters or gallops with each leg leading in turn, and so makes sure that the horse develops evenly on both sides.

The rider is on the right diagonal if he comes down into the saddle as the horse's right foreleg comes to the ground and on the left if he sits with that foreleg. So if he says 'Down' as he sits and watches the forelegs he will know which one he is on. To change from one to the other is easy, he merely sits for one extra step. Some old horses which have been ridden on the same diagonal all their lives will shy or stumble when the rider changes to throw him back on the one they have grown to prefer.

In the school the rider changes the diagonal every time he changes the rein, but here we come to a difficulty for the international experts disagree over which diagonal it is best to be on. Some feel they want to be sitting and using their maximum driving aids on the inside hind leg, others on the outside. However, they do agree that it is extremely important to ride on them both equally, so in dressage tests the rider may ride on the one he chooses provided he is consistent about it and changes over whenever he changes the rein. For schooling at home the rider must settle with himself which one he will ride on when going in each direction.

Turns on the forehand This is a dull but important exercise which must be taught to every four-year-old as soon as he is going freely round the school at the walk and trot and is obedient to both legs used together.

The object is to teach him to move away from one leg used alone and so gain control of his quarters. The practical uses of this are many; the horse becomes more controllable in traffic and he is more manœuvrable out hunting or in a party of horses, for his quarters can be turned away from those he might kick as he makes room for them to pass by. He becomes co-operative over opening gates and posting letters.

A good rider makes sure that every horse he owns understands the turn on the forehand and performs it willingly, but once it is learned there is no need to continue to practise it, for its use is purely practical and it does not supple the horse or improve his balance.

This movement is performed only from the halt, it is usual to make a half-turn and it is a good plan to walk on directly afterwards in order to maintain impulsion. Halting the horse parallel to a fence or wall will help to explain what is wanted. In the turn the horse moves the hind legs round in quiet, even steps while the inner foreleg marks time or pivots on the spot. In fact in the half-turn the horse will move his quarters round until he is facing in the opposite direction, but if a circle had been drawn round his forelegs they would still be inside it and they would never have left it. But to start with one step is enough and the horse should be patted and praised as he makes it.

To turn the quarters to the left the rider uses the right leg behind the girth, not in one continuous shove but with a press for each step to be taken. The left leg acts very quietly to keep the horse on the bit and control the number of steps. The hands have a complicated job; first they must tell the horse not to move forward, then if the right hand can feel the mouth and produce a slight flexion of the jaw the whole turn will be more supple and more elegantly executed. However the inexperienced rider is inclined to give too strong a rein aid, which confuses the horse, particularly if the hand is moved sideways, and makes him think he must move his *forehand* to the right, which is exactly what we wish to avoid. For this reason the inexperienced rider should merely use both hands to keep the horse still and his right leg to move the quarters round. He should sit up and look straight ahead.

If nothing happens the rider should keep calm and not apply wrong aids or lean over to one side or otherwise contort himself, as this will only make it more difficult and confusing for the horse. A tap with the long schooling whip behind the leg will usually have the right effect on a sensitive horse, but there are thick-skinned horses who ignore or even go against the leg. If this happens an assistant who can reinforce the rider's aid by pressing with the hand or, in extreme cases, prodding with the top of a whip is the best answer and if no assistant is available the rider should dismount and push the horse round himself as this will be much more effective than the sort of aids frustrated riders apply.

Saying 'Get over' and applying a light pressure of the hand to the horse's flank is an aid much used in the stable for moving the horse over when grooming or mucking out, and the trainer who teaches it to his young horse will have little trouble in teaching the turn on the forehand mounted.

As soon as the horse understands what is wanted the rider can concentrate on the details: the flexion of the jaw, the horse remaining steadily on the bit and, when moving to the left, the right hind leg crossing in front of the left which is a sign that impulsion is being maintained.

If the horse turns more easily to one side than the other teach him aids on the easy side and when he understands what is wanted practise more on the difficult side.

Shoulder-in When riding at the walk, trot, canter and gallop the horse's hind legs should follow exactly in the track of his forelegs and this applies whether he is on the straight, on a corner or circling. He must always be on *one* track. *Two* track work is taught because it is a wonderful schooling exercise; it supples the horse, it frees his shoulder, it engages the hind legs and makes him a lighter, less earthbound ride, capable of obeying finer aids.

To start with, shoulder-in is generally ridden on three tracks. Instead of his forelegs making one track and his hind legs another, as in the half pass, renvers and travers, we make it easier for him by asking for a less acute position.

If one side of the school has a hedge, wall or fence the rider should begin along this side. As he comes round the corner he continues the aids for turning so that the horse's head, neck and shoulder are all bent inwards, and then, with the outside rein, he shows him that he is to walk along the side of the school in this position. At first this aid will have to be rather pronounced and the outside hand should move away from the neck and *lead* him along the side of the school—he will naturally think that the inside rein is telling him to turn into the centre. Obviously tact is needed to explain this to the horse without upsetting him, and one step of the movement must be recognised, praised and rewarded by riding on straight.

The rider uses both legs to keep the horse on the bit and at first he may have to use the inside leg rather strongly. When the horse understands what is wanted the movement should become light and easy and ask the rider for no more effort than a circle.

The most usual mistake of the inexperienced rider is to use the hands backwards and bring the horse to a halt. If this happens he should be ridden on and the movement attempted with lighter rein aids when he again has impulsion. Another problem is the horse which obeys the inside rein and marches briskly into the centre of the school. This is usually due to a rider who finds it difficult to separate his hands and use them independently. The spoiled horse which objects to bending his body at all will need to practise more circling, and a slight shoulder-in position for a stride or two when circling is a good exercise for a horse that resists all attempts to bend him round the rider's inside leg.

Some riders make it very difficult for their horse to perform a shoulder-in by leaning against the movement. It is important to sit deep in the saddle, tall and straight above, and to look in the direction that you wish to go.

As usual it is best to teach the horse on the rein he finds easier and then work mostly on his stiff side later. At first the rider will concentrate on the bend and position of the horse but once this is established the important points to watch are whether the horse is using his inside hind leg powerfully. Is it crossing over the outside one? Has he relaxed and come on the bit?

Shoulder-in is a marvellous suppling and muscle-building exercise and should be practised regularly throughout the horse's life. It should be used when riding-in before a dressage test and to supple the horse before showjumping. It is the only movement in riding when the horse is asked to look in the opposite direction to the way he is going. When he can perform it at the walk it will do him even more good at the trot, but it is never ridden at the canter.

The halt A horse should always halt square, with his weight evenly distributed on all four legs, and on the bit. He should halt straight and stand quietly at attention until he receives the rider's next signal. With a young horse this will not all be achieved at once and it is a great mistake for the rider to become obsessed with the idea that the horse must stand square at any cost for this leads to fiddling with the hands and niggling with the heels and often produces a horse that won't stand at all.

The important point for the rider to watch is that he always gives the correct aids wherever he is and whatever he is doing; it is not enough just to give them in the school—they must become second nature to the rider. It must become unthinkable to him that he could ever *pull* his horse up.

At first all halts will be made from the walk. The rider stops his hands, slows his body and uses his legs and seat to ride the horse forward into the stopped hand. Since the walk is a pace of four-time and each leg has to make its own step the rider does not demand an immediate halt, but having given the signal tactfully allows the horse time to complete his sequence of steps and halt square.

Halting from the trot When the horse accepts the bit, goes with a steady head-carriage and has a rhythmical trot he can be asked to halt from it. This is a very good exercise especially for horses inclined to go on their forehands. The rider sits down and uses stronger leg, back and seat aids than for the halt from the walk. He can ask for a more immediate halt since the trot is a pace of two-time and only two steps make the stride.

The halt from the canter is a movement for the already well-trained horse, and is only required in the more advanced dressage tests.

The half halt This is an invaluable exercise for persuading the horse to carry more of his weight on his haunches, for producing impulsion and as a preparation and warning before making a transition. But the horse cannot make a half halt until he goes on the bit and is reasonably supple from jaw to hind leg. The rider, sitting very deep, uses his legs, back, seat and hands together as though he were about to halt from the trot, but as soon as the horse shortens the rider's hands give and so there is no change in the pace.

Apart from circles and transitions to the trot the half halt is the correct way to slow the canter. Any rider acquiring a spoiled horse and finding himself forced into riding with the brakes on, that is holding the horse back instead of riding it *forward* on to the bit, must set out to break the habit at once with circles and endless half halts. It doesn't matter how many half halts are used to control the spoiled horse, the rewarding action of the giving hand will have an effect in the end, whereas the deadening pressure of the perpetually tight rein can only destroy the horse's action and spoil his jumping, especially across country.

The transitions When changing from one pace to another the horse must remain balanced and on the bit, with a steady headcarriage and a relaxed jaw, and he must change directly from the pace he is in to the pace which is wanted without losing impulsion or shooting off in excitement.

When asked to canter from the trot the horse must not trot faster and faster, he must canter from the trot he is in at the moment the aid is given. Equally in the downward transitions his hind legs must be kept under him and he must not be allowed to fall or stumble into the slower pace and, as he moves off in it, impulsion must be maintained.

All the faults caused by lack of balance and impulsion must be dealt with by stronger use of the driving aids, the rider's legs back and seat; and then, as the horse becomes better schooled, they can usually be prevented by use of the preparatory half-halt.

Coming off the bit by throwing up the head or poking the nose can be caused by an over-severe rein aid and the rider should experiment to find out whether a lighter aid would do. The head coming up can also be a sign of the rider losing his seat and bumping on a weak-backed horse, or the horse may have been surprised by the suddenness of the demand. If so a warning half-halt can be given.

The horse that is frightened of his mouth, and so sets his jaw when he feels an aid coming, can sometimes be persuaded to stay relaxed and keep his jaw flexed by giving the rein on his stiff side a series of squeezes in time with the leg aid on the same side for the last few strides before the aid for the transition is given.

Rein back This movement is very useful in everyday life and so every horse should learn it. How early it should be taught depends on the individual horse, but there seems to be no reason why the young horse should not be taught to move back to the voice and pressure on the chest with a hand, just as he can get the idea of the turn on the forehand by being made to 'get over' in the stable.

All the difficulties and problems of reining back mounted are caused by the riders who will not think of it as a forward movement and are convinced they must pull on the reins. When they do this the horse's head goes up, his back stiffens and it becomes impossible for him to step back correctly in two-time, the legs moving in diagonal pairs as in the trot. All he can manage is small grudging steps, one leg at a time.

The rider must remind himself that it is a forward movement. Then, having halted, he moves both legs back slightly and presses with the calves. The horse begins to move forward but finds that the rider's hands have stopped. They are not pulling but they are not going with him as they would if he was to walk on. The rider says 'back' in a long drawn-out voice. If nothing happens the rider sends for an assistant who stands in front of the horse pressing him back or tapping him on the chest or knees. If there is no assistant available the rider teaches the horse what he wants dismounted. The horse can be faced to a wall, but it must be so high that it cannot conceivably be mistaken for a jump, as I have known dangerous misunderstandings over five-barred gates.

In a good rein back the horse remains calm and on the bit. He steps back straight, slowly but willingly, and he stops when he is asked.

The fussy temperamental horse which hates to stand still, and the horse which is behind the bit, should only practise this movement occasionally, but it is a very useful correction for the spoiled horse which tries to get his own way by throwing his weight on his forehand.

5

Elementary Jumping

Jumping lessons normally begin out hacking as the young horse follows the schoolmaster over uneven ground, and then over logs and banks and small ditches.

In the school the first fence is a pole on the ground and the crafty trainer accustoms his horse to brightly coloured poles at this stage. It is not very difficult to keep poles brightly painted or to change their colour schemes occasionally and it saves that irritating wail from eliminated competitors of 'My horse/pony isn't *used* to green/blue/purple poles'. A good trainer sees that his horse *is* used to them, for the poor horse cannot do anything about it.

When the horse walks and trots unconcernedly over a vividly painted pole on the ground, he can be introduced to cavalletti work. Poles placed on bricks or even on the ground can be used instead of cavalletti, but they are not as good for they roll when kicked and the rider will find himself perpetually dismounting to replace them.

CAVALLETTI WORK

Cavalletti work is a marvellous gymnastic exercise which develops the horse's muscles without overtaxing him; it teaches him to round his back and lower his head, thus assuming the correct shape for jumping; it teaches him to go calmly, to use his brain to work out strides and, what is more, most horses enjoy doing it, especially in company.

When the horse has walked over one cavalletti at the lowest height place a second one four foot away (four foot six if he is a large and long-striding horse); and keeping him long, low and relaxed walk over the two of them. The rider should look ahead, never down at the poles, and leave the horse to work out that it is done by placing a forefoot between the two of them. Usually the horse gets the idea very quickly at the walk; the trouble starts with the trot. Keep him walking for a day or two and increase the

Cavalletti work

number of cavalletti, up to six if you have them and the horse is going with complete confidence. Three is plenty for a worried horse. The best position for the cavalletti is either down the centre of the school or just outside the school track where they will not have to be moved to make room for circles and serpentines. It is important that they can be approached from either direction and on either rein without any tight turns which could unbalance the trotting horse for, once the work is learned, it will mostly be done at the trot.

At the trot we return to two cavalletti and we ride round the school and settle the horse into a very steady trot. He must be more or less on the bit and the rider must be riding forward. Some horses understand at once what is wanted, they plod round and round happily and on being given three cavalletti immediately round their backs and show a pronounced cadence—a moment of suspension in the step—for which they should be patted and praised and given a free walk as a reward.

Other horses, usually the weak-backed, excitable sort, fuss and worry and won't lower their heads and relax and so muddle their strides, trying something different every time. Others, usually older horses which have jumped, insist that they must hurl themselves over in an enormous leap.

The difficulty with both these problems is that the rider immediately feels that he *must* use the reins to hold the horse back or at least slow him up, and at once one of those vicious circles, which appear so frequently in riding, is set up. If the rider *does* use the reins the horse cannot lower his head and relax so he cannot stride over the cavalletti correctly. Hopeless though it seems, the rider *has* to change a situation where he wants to hold back into one where he is riding forward.

The first thing to try is substituting the voice for the reins. Having settled the horse in a steady trot, approach saying, 'Trot, trot, trot,' in calm commanding tones. If this fails, sometimes bringing the horse back to a walk just before the cavalletti and *then* riding forward convinces him that there is no need for wild leaps. The best cure of all is a schoolmaster horse which does not kick. Having let the youngster watch how it should be done several times, ride him over the cavalletti right on the schoolmaster's tail.

Once the horse has the idea the rider can think of his own position. He can ride at either the rising or sitting trot, with either the dressage or jumping seat but he must go with the horse and follow him with the hands, not throwing the reins away; but following, giving the horse the exact amount of rein he asks for as he stretches out his neck. The rider must use his legs quietly and in time with the horse's stride; there must be no kicking for that would disturb him. The need to kick or to steer with the reins or the fact that the horse runs out are all signs that he is not on the bit, and he should be taken away and got going properly before the cavalletti are attempted again.

We do not want the horse to associate jumping with kicking, whacking and refusals, but many riders allow this to happen because they permit idleness elsewhere and expect a miraculous transformation at the sight of a fence. Just a few horses love jumping so much that this happens, even in shows, but the great majority only offer the standard of impulsion and obedience that their trainers extract when schooling on the flat.

When the horse trots well over the cavalletti more can gradually be added, up to six in all, and it may be possible to widen the distance between them to five feet; we want the horse to take a long stride, but not one that is an effort for him.

Cavalletti work is such a good exercise for both horse and rider that it can be practised for five or ten minutes several times a week. Horses of Olympic Three Day Event standard use it for suppling and muscling up.

CAVALLETTI AND JUMP

The next stage is to introduce a small fence, about two-foot-six high and place it nine to twelve feet from the last of the cavalletti. The idea of this exercise is that the horse is in the right shape for jumping and the rider can sit quietly without 'steering' and let the horse carry him over. We want to avoid any busyness or bossiness on the part of the rider, any suggestion that the horse has to be 'got over'. The rider who uses maximum strength, aids and determination to jump two-foot-six will have nothing in reserve when confronted by a fifteen-foot brook.

FOUR JUMPS

When the last exercise is accomplished calmly and easily by horse and rider, four small jumps are collected and arranged on the diagonals of the school. The cavalletti can be used at their top height with extra poles and oil drums to make them look a little more imposing and about two foot six in height. It is important that all jumps should look solid and not fall easily. Flimsy poles with large spaces under them or between them are very bad schooling jumps for young horses, who must be taught to respect their fences and helped to find their take-offs with plenty of filling in. This can be supplied by oil drums, crossed poles,

bundles of brushwood or a pole on the ground providing a
straightforward ground-line.

SPREAD FENCES

Since schooling over spread fences produces a better jumper with
greater scope and style and fluency, the wise trainer builds more
spread fences than straight ones, especially in the early stages of
his schooling, and he makes sure that the elements nearer to the
horse are carefully graduated in height, becoming lower and

Popping over

lower, as this will help him to find his take-off and encourage
him to stand back.

A triple for instance is a very much easier jump for a young
horse than a parallel. A brush fence with an oxer rail on the far
side is much simpler than one with the rails on the take-off side.
At this stage the width of a fence should not be greater than its
height.

APPROACHING

The horse has to do the jumping but it is the rider's job to organise
the approach, particularly when he has walked or built the course

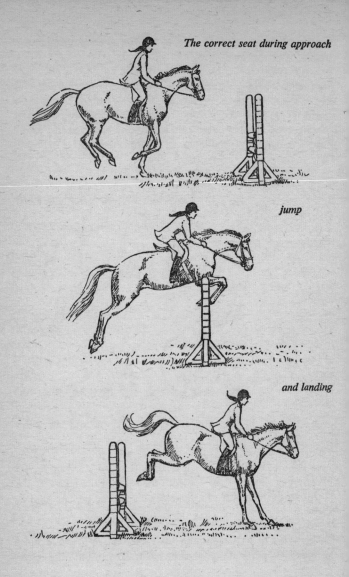

The correct seat during approach

jump

and landing

and knows what lies ahead and the horse does not. So during the approach the rider, by his adjustment of speed impulsion and contact, influences the take-off and gives the trained horse valuable information about the fence, but the horse is the one who takes off. With the inexperienced horse a mass of meaningless signals will only confuse him, so we build helpful, easy jumps. We approach slowly so that he is balanced and has time to think, but riding forward so that he has impulsion and an active hind leg ready to propel him over. We sit very still, just sending him on with the legs, remembering that small movements on the part of the rider distract him from choosing his take-off and large ones unbalance him. Hitting and kicking in the three strides before the take-off *cause* refusals.

If a young horse is afraid of a fence he should be walked up quietly and allowed to look at it; if he is going badly without impulsion or he is napping he should be taken away and schooled. The approach to a fence must not be a battle-ground where all the unresolved problems of our schooling are fought out.

TAKING OFF

The horse should take off the height of the fence away: three feet from a three foot fence, four feet from a four foot one. If he has exceptional scope he may take off further back, up to the height and a half of the fence and the rider must learn to adapt to this; but if the horse takes off nearer to the jump than the height of it he will either knock it down or he will have to go straight up in the air. This will cost him a much greater effort and give him less pleasure than jumping well.

The horse looks at the bottom of the fence when he measures his take-off, and that is why ground lines are so important and why false ones must never be used except for extremely experienced horses.

At one time there was a fashion for giving a sharp kick on the take-off. Arriving at the wrong moment this kick of course produced disastrous results, but even if given at the right time it caused the willing jumper to go faster and flatter. Our aim, particularly at this stage, is to go slowly, and rounded. As for the idle horse, well, kicking is a great deadener of feeling and the horse that *is* kicked soon becomes the horse that *has* to be kicked. Kicking, like shouting, should be kept for emergencies and it will then have some effect.

POPPING OVER

Having arranged his four small jumps the rider shortens his stirrups and trots round the school with the jumping seat. When he has the horse going well he inclines inward from a quarter marker and pops over one of the jumps. He then trots on in a calm and unconcerned manner and, presently, if the horse is going well, he turns in and jumps another.

When the horse is absolutely calm about jumping one fence he can try two. He should approach at the trot but if he canters the last stride this does not matter provided he comes back to a trot after each fence. If he becomes unbalanced the rider must not use rough aids nor must he ride on at the next fence: he must turn the horse away and circle or ride round the school until he has him balanced and on the bit again.

It may be tempting to go on. The jumps are small, the horse will obviously get over, but at this stage we are trying to lay the foundations of a really good jumper; we do not want just to get over. Our sights are set on clear rounds across country or in the ring and we want to make good style, calmness, obedience, the correct bend round corners habitual to our horse before we come to large fences or important events.

Of course it is easier to have one fence, or perhaps two in a straight line, and just to jump backwards and forwards over them, raising them occasionally until we find out how high the horse can jump. But, though we may discover that he has the aptitude to jump five feet this will not do the horse much good, nor the rider in the long run. An ability to jump clear rounds, perhaps three in one competition, is what we are trying to produce, not the ability to take a flying leap over one large fence.

Besides the fact that our four-jump, figure-of-eight course

teaches horse and rider to remain balanced and to make use of the whole ring, the ability to jump slowly but with impulsion is extremely important. Out hunting and in horse trials there are always fences which demand a slow approach, because of steep ground, or tight turns, or limited space or sometimes simply because the amount of information that the horse has to gather about the fence cannot be assimilated in a fast approach. The horse that will creep or pop or gallop on at his fences is the one we want to produce.

TEACHING COURAGE

A large part of courage is self-confidence and this part can be built up, or diminished, by riding and training. A horse that has jumped a wide variety of tiny jumps will feel himself capable of tackling a wide variety of jumps of whatever height he is capable at every stage of training. This does not mean that a complete set of show jumps is necessary, though of course the more jumps you possess the better, but if you have only four ingenuity can multiply them into many more.

Coloured blankets, weighted down with stones in windy weather, are a very easy way of transforming plain poles. Exotically painted oil drums, plastic buckets, washing-up bowls, or rows of gum-boots placed under fences give them a new look. Macintoshes and plastic sheeting, well anchored down, as well as sacks and horse rugs, can be draped on jumps. Old doors or planks, painted to look like bricks, can be used below poles to simulate walls. Gaily coloured garden chairs can be placed as wings, umbrellas tied to posts to make canopied pillars.

There is no end to what can be done, but of course the jumps must be kept small, the poles must be solid and there must be nothing which could trap or frighten the horse should he make a mistake. Also at this stage the fences must be kept wide and anything like a bench or table with a false ground-line must have a true ground-line added.

Obviously all these new horrors should not be introduced at once. One strange fence per lesson will do, and there should be no feeling that the horse has to be 'got over'. You want to produce the sort of horse that *carries* you over and you will not do that by kicking and beating.

If a horse is horrified by a new jump ride him up to it quietly, or, if he will not approach, dismount and lead him up. Touch the horror yourself, telling him that it is perfectly safe, and, if necessary step backwards and forwards over it yourself pointing out that it is perfectly jumpable. The great thing about teaching courage over tiny jumps is that they can be dismantled to stepping-over height.

COMBINATIONS

Having taught the horse to jump small single fences confidently, whatever their shape and colour, the trainer now moves on to combinations and teaching the horse to adjust, and to have confidence in his ability to adjust, his stride.

The young horse should never be worried by two problems at once so the fences again become plain familiar ones, leaving him free to concentrate on working out his stride.

At this stage of training the trainer does not interfere with the stride for the horse is not sufficiently suppled for the half-halt to go through, and the combinations are built so that the only demand they make is for impulsion. They should ask only that the horse is going forward and will lengthen his stride and go on, never that he should check or shorten his stride. For this reason a spread fence will always follow a straight fence in a double and never the other way round. The rider can then start at a trot, jump the straight fence and ride on at the spread. There is no worry about making the horse stand back, no temptation to use the hands, which at this stage of schooling would cause a loss of impulsion. When the double has been mastered and a treble is attempted the bigger spread will be the last fence and the distance between the second and third fences will be the same or longer than between the first two.

The horse will now be cantering on at the second and third fences, but he should still begin at the trot, for most young horses cannot maintain a balanced canter for long, and they gradually collapse on to their forehands as they tire. We do not want this to happen in the middle of the combination, as it will cause him to make a bad jump, bang his legs or refuse.

DISTANCES

The distances between jumps in combinations should be made easy for young and novice horses, because we want them to come 'right' without a lot of interference from the rider. The difficulty is that our horse may be from fourteen to seventeen hands and have a long, short or medium stride for his size. Since we want the young horse to go forward at all costs it is better to have the distances too long rather than too short, but with very low fences, where the horse is popping rather than jumping, he will be taking off and landing much closer than over large fences, and so distances need to be reduced a little.

If the fences are over three feet most horses find twenty-five feet for one stride and thirty-five for two easy distances. A fourteen-hand pony will probably find it possible to fit one stride in at twenty-one feet and no stride at eighteen feet whereas a large horse would regard eighteen feet as a trap and manage twenty-one feet without a stride.

With a young horse one should build combinations with the distances one thinks will suit him and alter them if they do not. And, since later on the information will be very useful in competitions, one should make a mental note of what distances are easy or difficult for him and how many strides he puts in.

GRID-JUMPING

Cavalletti work at the canter or grid-jumping is another excellent exercise for teaching the horse to adjust his stride. The cavalletti are used at either their second or top height and arranged eight feet apart for small ponies, nine to ten feet for fourteen-twos and ten to twelve feet for horses. The essentials are now to maintain impulsion, to look ahead and to ride only at the canter, for the distances are now impossible for good jumping at the trot. If the horse canters, the stride will automatically come right, and if impulsion is maintained and the rider looks ahead there will be no need to steer with the reins and no risk of running out. Six cavalletti are generally used.

Grid-jumping is particularly good for the cumbersome horse with a ponderous stride, or for horses that lack confidence or impulsion. It is not so good for the over-confident tearaway,

Cantering over cavalletti

and once he has learned to grid-jump he should go back to doing his cavalletti work at the trot.

PENS

Pens, which can be built from cavalletti to start with, are another good training jump. As they grow larger they should be built with an opening so that the apprehensive horse can be trotted in and popped out and the over-confident can be asked to jump it in a different manner every time he is put at it, which will make him listen to his rider and wait for orders.

Angles Once the horse is completely confident over jumping fences straight he can be popped over them from angles. Only a very slight angle at first and care should be taken not to surprise him or present him at the jump unbalanced. Large fences must not be jumped from an angle until the horse is experienced and will stand back when asked and the rider must always consider the extra width of a spread fence when taken on a slant and not confront his horse with anything impossible.

COURSES

When the horse jumps readily from the trot and canter, when he enjoys the challenge of combinations and takes on the most horrific-looking jumps after one stop for examination, he is ready for a course. A cross-country course, or a semi-cross-country course built round the outside of your field, is usually better for a young horse than a showjumping one. The extra space between the fences gives time to restore lost balance and introduces an element of fun and excitement. The faster pace suits the half-schooled horse whose hind legs are not yet strong enough for collection, and, since the rider has fewer worries about tight turns, he will be less likely to misuse the reins and impulsion will be easier to maintain.

If the horse goes well and remains balanced he should be ridden straight round at an even pace, and as his blood rises he will enjoy the challenge of meeting the unknown fence, making an instant decision and flying over; he will become bold, which is an important attribute in a cross-country horse.

But should either horse or rider feel apprehensive, or should the horse get unbalanced or begin to take off wildly, it is better to come back to a trot, or circle between the fences, and to take each individually as a separate jump. Sometimes if one starts like this the horse's confidence builds up as he goes round and he will begin to suggest going on.

Some tearaways settle down on cross-country courses and go well, partly because the rider feels more able to ride forward when he has plenty of space and so there is nothing to fight. If, however, the excitable horse gets his head up and starts taking off rashly he should be circled and put back on the bit. In competitions one takes a chance if one comes at a fence wrong or unbalanced, but when schooling the merit is not in getting over but in how it was done. Also, we do not want to risk unnerving the horse by banging his legs or giving him a fall.

Going across country in pairs or groups is an excellent school for the horse which lacks confidence and for the idle and steady, but it is not so good for the tearaway unless he is put in the lead.

FREE JUMPING

A horse can be taught to jump without a rider either in a jumping lane or on the lunge. And then there is the Irish method of leading the horse across country on the lunge and sending someone behind him with a whip.

All these methods have their uses but none of them do the actual work of producing a well-schooled, obedient jumper who though bold and confident is attentive to his rider.

With the jumping lane the horse is put in at the top, goes down the jumps completely free, and is retrieved at the bottom. This can be of use to the horse which lacks confidence, but it does the tearaway no good at all and makes the over-confident horse even less inclined to listen to his rider.

The Irish method can be very useful with horses which hate water or ditches. It is extremely difficult to sit still on a horse that is teetering hysterically on the brink of a ditch or stream and this means that the rider's weight is tipping about and probably unbalancing the horse when he does attempt to take off. If he is put on the lunge and his rider steps over the obstacle the horse may gather up enough courage to follow. If he does not, an assistant with the whip can be useful, but he should not be too noisy or aggressive; too much whip-brandishing can take the horse's mind off the jump.

Jumping on the lunge proper can be very useful if a horse is off work with a bad back, or if his rider is incapacitated. It can also be helpful if a good horse starts to refuse for no apparent reason, as it enables the rider to study his horse and decide whether the change is due to pain or stiffness in the horse's back or legs, or whether it may be due to his own riding. Sometimes a rider does change his style without noticing; he may take up too strong a contact or too short a rein, or he may be dropping his hands on the take-off. If a horse refusing with a rider is full of confidence without one the rider must obviously suspect himself.

CONCLUSION

The objects of the early jumping lessons are to produce a horse which is confident, calm and obedient, which enjoys jumping and very, very rarely refuses; a horse which will jump a small course smoothly and in good style with the rider riding forward, using light leg aids, but sitting still and quiet. Kicking, shouting and beating, refusing and running out are all signs of an inefficient trainer. The height at which the horse is now jumping should be from two-foot-nine to three-foot-three, but at this stage it is confidence and style that matter. If the horse has the ability to jump high, good training will bring it out; if he has not there is nothing that the trainer can do about it, except find him a home where his ability to jump small jumps well will be appreciated.

The greatest mistake a trainer can make is to overface his horse and cause him to lose confidence by confronting him with fences that are too large or too complicated. And mismanagement of the approach can also have the same effect if it leads to banged legs and falls.

The second mistake is to sour the horse and make him hate jumping by repeating the same course time and again, or by asking him to jump higher and higher. Going backwards and forwards over the same fences is extremely boring for a horse, but all jumping is an effort and working out how to take unknown fences is a mental strain; so the rider must limit himself. He must make it plain to the horse that a clear round is a moment for praise and rejoicing and also a *rest*. And if later he wants to put a few jumps up, try a combination again with a slightly longer stride, that is fine, but the horse whose rider never shows that he is pleased, never seems content with a good round and *stops*, will gradually become sour, and the more effort the jumps are to him the quicker this will happen.

The third mistake a trainer can make is to expect impulsion and obedience when jumping if he has not insisted upon it when hacking or schooling on the flat. Chapter 5 will not be successful unless the work described in Chapter 4 is being carried out efficiently at the same time, and the horse is being ridden properly out hacking.

As the year passes and the young horse improves, the trainer will be more and more tempted to enter for shows and horse trials. Perhaps there will be some local event of a very novice standard with small, well-built jumps which could prove a useful school. The horse may go well and the rider will then have to resist the temptation to compete in endless jumps-off, or to cut corners riding against the clock. He must remember that it is often the good horses which are spoiled and that those under five should not really be appearing in public at all.

6

Advanced Schooling

When a horse has reached his fifth birthday, provided he is fit and well and has done the preliminary work described in earlier chapters, he can begin to work harder and learn the more demanding exercises.

Older horses which have been ridden but not schooled must also be put through the whole curriculum; to begin half-way would be the equivalent of asking an untrained person to carry out advanced ballet movements. It is not enough to be grown up and intelligent, you have to have suppled and developed the right muscles by practising the easier exercises. The development of the muscles cannot be hurried; a four-year-old takes a a year over his preliminary work and older horses may manage it in three months, but try to cram it into one month and you are likely to end with an irritable and unco-operative horse resentful over aching muscles.

There is a great danger of this happening when a horse is sent away to be schooled. The owner expects quick results, the professional trainer does his best to provide them and the poor horse suffers. Head-shaking, tongue over the bit, going behind the bit and over-bending are all ways in which a suffering horse will try to escape the discomforts of a too-rapid education. As an owner you should always make it clear to any stable or person who takes your horse for a week or two before the start of the holidays that you realise that there will be no miraculous transformation and that the horse is chiefly there to get fit.

THE CANTER

With our five-year-old who has been cantering out hacking and round the field and offering us better and better transitions to the trot as time has passed, we now begin to canter round the school. This is hard work and not for the grass-fed or the thick winter coat and, since the tired horse collapses on his forehand at the canter, it is a waste of time to attempt the work on an unfit horse.

Out hacking we have asked the horse to canter with a particular leading leg, so that he should not get into the habit of always favouring one. We have used the diagonal aids: for the off fore we have felt the right rein, used the right leg on the girth and the left leg slightly stronger further back. We have done this from the sitting trot, which gives more opportunity to use the seat and back and also because, later on, we will be teaching the extended trot and the fact that we are rising or not rising will become a valuable signal in telling the horse which movement we want.

Since the sequence of the canter with the off fore leading is near hind, near fore and off hind together and then the off fore, or, in other words, the first leg to the ground is the diagonally opposite hind leg and the last is the leading leg itself, we use the left leg to set the near hind in motion and start the sequence which will end with the appearance of the leading leg itself. Bending the horse's head inwards with the inside hand and starting on a corner or circle have all helped the young horse to understand what we required and he should canter happily with either leg leading.

The rider now has to teach the horse to obey a lighter and lighter aid, partly because the use of the outside leg is inclined to make him swing his quarters, partly because the diagonal aids are needed for two-track work and to use them for the canter as well will cause confusion, but mainly because strong aids used repeatedly make a sensitive horse irritable. The aids now become a light feel on the rein which asks for a flexion of the jaw on the side of the leading leg. A flexion is a relaxation, a slight opening of the horse's mouth and it shows that he accepts the bit and is at the rider's disposal (he cannot do this if he has one of those lunatic riders who pull their drop nosebands tight). Having warned the horse which leg is wanted the rider sits down and with both legs seat and back asks for the canter. Another refinement is to move the seat bone on the side of the leading leg very slightly forward, this will enable the rider to sit closer to the horse during the canter and also makes the aids more plain.

SLOWING THE CANTER

With a young horse the school, the circle and the transitions will usually produce the slower but still active canter that we want; with a spoiled horse the half-halt will be needed as well. The rider canters round the school and on a twenty-metre circle, and he must always have the feeling that though he is going slowly he is riding forward, never that he is holding the horse back. He changes the rein diagonally across the school with a simple change of leg through the trot.

When the horse does all this smoothly and calmly he practises the transitions from trot to canter and canter to trot round the school, at this stage always leading with the inside leg. The horse must stay on the bit throughout the transition, neither throwing up his head nor collapsing on his forehand, and if he is happy and calm he can do six starts on one rein followed by six on the other. If he shows signs of irritability, ears back, swishing tail or swinging quarters, the rider may be using aids that are too severe or riding with a contact that is too strong. If he lightens the aids and finds that the horse is still irritable then it must be assumed that the work is too difficult and he should be taken back a stage. A horse is never improved by endlessly practising what makes him unhappy and upset for, if the fault does lie with him, it is almost certainly due to conformation or muscular problems and the answer is to try to overcome the difficulty with an easier exercise.

CANTERING FROM THE WALK

When the trot-canter transition is perfect, the walk to canter and canter to walk transitions can be practised. These transitions will require a stronger use of the rider's seat and back than those to and from the trot. But if the rider finds himself using rough aids or throwing his body about in an attempt to start the canter he will know that the horse is not yet ready for the work.

THE PIROUETTE or TURN ON THE HAUNCHES

This movement can be performed from the halt or on the move. From the halt the horse moves his forehand round in quiet, even steps while his hind legs either mark time on the spot or the inner hind leg may pivot. In the pirouette on the move there must be no pivoting and the hind legs must mark time in the cadence of the pace; but this is difficult and belongs to advanced dressage.

The aids for a turn to the right are: the right rein leads the horse's forehand to the right supported by the left rein (a supporting hand comes up to the wither but must not cross it). The left leg, just behind the girth, controls the quarters and stops them swinging to the left, which would make a turn on the centre instead of on the haunches, the right leg, on the girth, maintains impulsion. When teaching the movement it is best to halt beside a wall or fence, as this will help to explain to the horse that he is not to swing his quarters, and to ask for only a quarter turn instead of the usual half. When a quarter turn is made from the school track the horse will be facing inwards and he should be ridden straight forward and not turned back to the track which will confuse him.

Some horses get the idea at once, others seem incapable of understanding what is wanted. As usual it is pointless to upset the horse or to apply the lunatic aids of the frustrated; one has to try to explain better. With a wall of fence beside one it is possible to take the left leg from its duty of controlling the quarters and to use it further forward to help push the forehand round, provided one only asks for a quarter turn, after that the quarters are free from the wall and will certainly escape. This is not an orthodox aid, but it can help to explain matters to the horse. Once the movement is understood the rider can walk round the school either making the turns from the half-halt or from a just made halt. In this way he will be better able to maintain impulsion than if he had been standing for some time.

TWO TRACK WORK

The next two movements, renvers and travers, can be taught either before or after the turn on the haunches and if the horse is inclined to lose impulsion it is probably better to teach them first.

TRAVERS or HEAD TO WALL

In travers the horse is bent along his whole body as though he was circling and then ridden along the side of the school in this position with his head to the wall. It is *not* like shoulder-in. For the horse is bent and flexed in the direction in which he is going, his head leads the movement and the rider should just see his inside

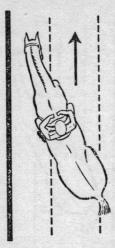

Travers

eye; this makes it more difficult for both horse and rider. With a schooled horse the angle to the wall should be 45 degrees, but at first this would call for too much effort so an angle of 30 degrees should be aimed at.

The best way to begin a left travers would be to circle on the left rein or to come round a corner, and on joining the track to keep the position and proceed along the track with the horse's head to the wall. The left rein, supported by the right, will take him to the left and the right leg just behind the girth, pushes him to the left; the right leg maintains impulsion. The rider sits up and looks where he is going. A step or two is enough at first, and impulsion

and the sideways movement are more important than the position
of the head, which can be sorted out later.

RENVERS or TAIL TO WALL

This is the same movement as travers but carried out the opposite
way round with the horse's tail to the wall, or school track,
instead of his head. Experts disagree about which is the easier to
teach first. Renvers has a more complicated start, as on joining
the track from a corner or circle the rider has to change his aids

Renvers

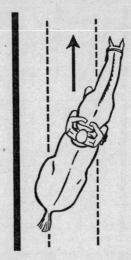

and the horse's bend for, having turned the horse inwards and
put his tail in the right place, he now has to get him bent and
flexed in the direction in which he is going. Once this problem of
adopting the correct position is mastered I think renvers becomes
the easier to perform.

Both these movements can be ridden at the walk, trot and canter
on the straight, and are particularly enjoyable at the canter. They
are good for all horses and ought to be much more widely taught
and practised; though difficult for the rider at first they will make
him a far more accomplished horseman.

THE HALF PASS

The half pass differs from renvers and travers in that the horse moves forwards and sideways at the same time and his body is not bent, but his head should still lead the movement and he should have a slight flexion on the side to which he is going. Because he has to go forwards and sideways the half pass is always performed diagonally across the school. In the half pass to the right the horse is shown the way with the right hand supported by the left, and

Half pass to the left   *Half pass to the right*

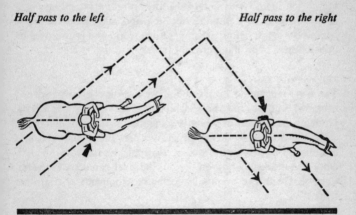

the left leg sends the horse sideways while the right keeps him moving forward. Pace, impulsion and sideways movement are important at first, and the bend and flexion of the head and neck can be corrected later. It is a fault for the quarters to lead the movement, and this can be caused by the rider giving an unnecessarily strong leg aid. The rider must sit straight and look where he is going, and he must not lean in the opposite direction to the movement.

A long half pass from quarter marker to quarter marker is tiring so it is usual to begin by turning down the centre of the school and half passing back to the track. Later on when the horse is efficient the counter change of hand is a very pleasant movement to ride; the change of bend at x needs a couple of strides on the straight and a skilful change of aids.

The half pass can be performed at the trot and canter and is particularly enjoyable at these paces, but it must be taught at the walk.

THE FULL PASS

This movement, when the horse moves sideways without gaining forward ground, is not suitable for the ordinary riding horse as it is too difficult to maintain impulsion and may drive the horse behind the bit. It belongs to high school work, and is also used by police horses controlling crowds.

THE VARIOUS TROTS

The trots recognised by the F.E.I. were ordinary, collected and extended, but they have now included the Working trot which the Germans have used for many years under the name of *mitteltrab*.

As the horse's schooling progresses and the ordinary trot is established as a cheerful, active, rhythmical pace with no difficulty about keeping him on the bit, the rider can start the variations that will lead eventually to the developments of the other trots.

The extended trot must show a lengthening of stride. Quickening the stride is useless, and if the horse does this he must be brought back to the ordinary trot and his quarters made more active by a circle or shoulder-in before another attempt to extend is made. If the horse extends for a few strides he should be praised, and too much must not be asked of him at first, for extension does demand a very powerful use of the hind legs.

The collected trot is slower than the ordinary trot, but it must be very powerful and the horse must carry himself proudly. Here again circling will be useful in producing the active action of the hind legs that is needed. But it must remain a true rhythmical pace, the uneven prancings of the rider who has produced more impulsion than he can sit on or control are as bad as the dispirited shuffle offered by the rider who has put his horse behind the bit.

The new working trot is really the beginning of the extended trot. The horse lengthens his stride while remaining short and almost collected, with his head high and his nose approaching the vertical and proceeds at about the speed of the ordinary trot, but he does not extend his neck and body, he does not change his shape as he must for the extended trot.

Small ponies and horses with poor natural action find it almost impossible to produce any real extension of stride, but luckily this is of no great importance as the movement is only asked for in fairly advanced dressage tests—though this will include the open horse trial horse.

The rider usually rises for the extended and sits for the collected trot.

COLLECTION IN GENERAL

All this work and all these exercises should have developed a horse with very powerful hind legs and, as they come further and further under his body and carry more and more of his and his rider's weight, his body will shorten in the slower paces and his head carriage will become higher. He will be light in front, and this combined with his dropped nose and relaxed jaw will give the rider effortless rein control; this is collection. But the horse must also remain capable of extension, of galloping and, above all, of stretching out and taking up all the rein he is offered at the loose rein walk. If he loses these abilities as his schooling advances, he is behind the bit and not collected.

A horse should flex from the poll as well as in the jaw, but the poll must always remain the highest part of the head-carriage. If the horse appears to be going on the bit and the top part of the neck is higher than the poll then he is overbending. This is a very serious fault for, if it is continued for long, it will stop the hind legs working and lead to a total lack of impulsion.

The German showjumping riders do overbend their horses just before jumping, but this is only a momentary exercise to impress the correct rounded shape on the horses and stop them from jumping flat. Being very strong riders, they have no difficulty in producing impulsion afterwards.

There is another form of overbending that can appear as the horse starts collected work. If we draw a line from the front plane of the horse's face vertically to the ground, the horse's nose should always be in advance of it. The high school horse's head may become vertical momentarily in extreme collection, but never behind the vertical, for this would be to refuse contact with the bit and so be out of the rider's control.

THE COLLECTED WALK

All collection has its dangers, but the collected walk is the most dangerous pace as it is the most difficult at which to maintain impulsion. It is better not to practise the collected walk on an ordinary riding horse, but just to assume it for a moment when it is needed, say before a turn on the haunches. All collection should be practised in short spells, and afterwards the horse should be given a loose rein walk to allow him to relax and stretch out.

THE COLLECTED CANTER

The collected canter must not be forced; it will come of itself as the rider practises starts from the walk and two-track work and, as it develops, it should be alternated with the extended canter. A good exercise is to use the collected canter for the short sides of the school and the extended canter down the long sides, always watching that the horse lengthens his neck, body and, particularly, stride. He should devour the ground with long strides rather than just increase his speed, and to allow this the rider has to increase the length of the rein.

THE CHANGE OF LEG

There come moments in schooling when the ways divide and one has to make decisions about one's horse's future career. The change of leg and the counter-canter bring us to one of these points.

With the hunter, the showjumper, the polo and gymkhana pony we want a mount full of initiative who will change his leading leg whenever *he* thinks fit. The rider will be busy, he will not want to have to give an aid, so we aim to produce a horse that is light and balanced, equally happy on either leg and has absolutely no inhibition about changing, but does it instinctively on every turn.

The advanced dressage horse has a very different scene. He must *never* change legs unless he receives an aid to do so.

In between there is the horse trial horse who may be called upon to perform a dressage test which includes the counter-canter and yet has to change on his own initiative in the showjumping and cross country. He is taught to change legs unless he receives an aid *not* to do so, and this is the most difficult situation of the three.

THE COUNTER-CANTER

In this movement the rider asks the horse to canter round corners, circles and curves with the outside leg leading. It is an advanced suppling exercise, leads up to the change of leg and is required in dressage tests once the horse is out of novice classes. It must not be confused with the disunited canter; this is a faulty pace in which the horse's legs move in an incorrect sequence and is usually caused by the horse changing in front and not behind. It is a serious fault and the horse should be stopped at once and restarted. Before attempting the counter-canter we practise starts from the walk again, but this time we mix the leading legs, asking for them at random to make sure that the horse is watching for and obeying the aids and not guessing which leg he will be asked for next. If the rider comes to a corner with the outside leg leading he stops, because a slight curve at the counter canter is all we must ask at first. If the rider is cantering down the long side of the school on the right rein with the near fore leading, he will gradually curve inwards using the right rein to give the direction but keeping the flexion of the jaw to the leading leg with the left rein. This obviously needs skilful handling of the reins, but it should be no problem to anyone who has mastered work on two tracks. It is, however, almost impossible if the rider has not achieved control of the hind quarters and is using the reins to slow the horse. The rider must sit very still and be careful not to change his seat in the saddle, for this would amount to an aid for the change of leg.

When the horse is calm and relaxed over curves he can be asked for a slight serpentine down the centre line, and over the weeks this serpentine can be deepened. But, at the slightest sign of stiffness the work must be made easier, and if the horse does change the rider must correct him very gently and show no sign of impatience. The horse is being asked to do something that appears difficult and unnatural to him and great tact is needed. Later, when the horse is accomplished at serpentines, circles, corners and figures of eight can all be ridden at the counter canter.

THE CHANGE OF LEG ON DEMAND

The flying change on demand is a very difficult dressage movement; it must be carried out when the horse is in the 'air' and has no legs on the ground between the third beat of the canter and before the sequence starts again with the first beat of the next stride. The movement must be balanced and straight; swinging a horse off balance to make him change is bad riding and may cause him to canter disunited.

The simple change of leg with a stride at either the walk or trot is the correct method of changing on demand on any but an advanced dressage horse. As I have already said the horse changes legs naturally on a change of direction and for most riding horses this ability is better not inhibited. In other words do not bother with the counter-canter or the flying change on demand unless you are entering for competitions which require them.

Before the change is attempted the horse must be perfectly happy at the counter-canter and with starts from the walk, and be capable of a high degree of collection.

The aids to change, a reversal of the rein and seat bone aids already in use, have to be given before the horse is in the air, usually as the leading leg appears, but this depends slightly on the reaction time of the particular horse. At first the change will be made on a change of direction, say on rejoining the track after a loop; later they can be made on a straight line.

Too many changes at first can go to the horse's head, so the work must not be over-practised, and it is important to keep up the counter-canter to prevent him anticipating aids to change.

We have been schooling our horse in a forty-metre by twenty-metre area, and as this is the size of all arenas until you reach the adult 'M' test the enlargement to a sixty by twenty space will be no problem. But the boards which surround the arena often have an inhibiting effect on inexperienced horses and riders and so must not be met for the first time in a competition. The good trainer always seizes every opportunity to school his young horse in a proper dressage arena and not just to practise the test. If no arena is available the trainer must do his best to simulate one by boxing his school in with cavalletti and jumping poles. If the supply is limited the corners should be boxed in and then as much of the sides as is possible. It is also important to accustom the horse to D, X and G by marking them on the ground with large splodges of whitewash. Otherwise a horse going in early in a competition, when they are still visible, may shy away or even try to jump them and so lose valuable points. Never enter or leave an arena by stepping over the boards or the horse may feel entitled to do so when it suits him; always use the entrance at A.

The dressage test is an examination. It is carefully designed to test the horse's schooling and to expose the faults of horse and rider. The judges award marks for each movement according to the official scale: Excellent 10; Very Good 9; Good 8; Fairly Good 7; Satisfactory 6; Sufficient 5; Insufficient 4; Fairly Bad 3; Bad 2; Very Bad 1; Not Performed 0. But the inexperienced competitor does not always realize that these marks take into account the basic correctness of the horse, as well as his performance of the particular movement. If the horse has a stiff back and is off the bit he cannot get more than four, and his errors will be deducted from four, while the supple, well-schooled horse will have his errors deducted from the eight or nine to which his correct basic training entitles him. Having said this it must be added that accuracy and attention to detail can collect the points needed to win when competing against equals and that a quiet, intelligently ridden, neat test almost always comes out higher than the ragged excitable one.

Probably the best advice one can give the novice is to ride slowly and deliberately and to try to carry out the movements accurately, but not to ask the horse to give his best. This will only worry and upset him and the horse which 'boils over' comes out with the lowest marks of all.

ENTERING

While the rider awaits the signal to begin he walks round outside the boards, and when the car horn is tooted or the bell rung he must not grab the reins or kick the horse in the ribs and make a disorganised and flurried entry, he has to force himself to stay calm and relaxed.

It is difficult to enter exactly on the centre line for A is in the way, but the rider must come past A on a slight slant and then manœuvre himself onto the line as he enters. This manœuvre should be practised at home with a friend standing at C to report on its success; the horse should hide A from the judges. It is important to enter deliberately and with impulsion. Wavering and the need to steer will both lose marks. The rider should fix his eyes on some point above the judges and ride towards it. He should not look down for X but, by watching E or B out of the corner of an eye, know when he has reached it. The halt should be smooth and straight, and once it is made the rider should not niggle at the horse or try to improve upon it. Male riders salute by putting the reins in the left hand and removing the hat with an elegant sweep. Female riders put the reins in the left hand and bow sweeping the right hand back in an elegant gesture. If the horse has halted well and is standing like a rock the rider should take his time and give the judge plenty of opportunity to observe this accomplished performance. But if the halt was crooked with trailing hocks, or the horse is refusing to stand, the salute should be brisk and the rider should pass on rapidly to better things.

Novices are sometimes so overcome by the occasion that they stop using the inside leg and, ceasing to go into the corners, use only the middle of the arena. If it is the horse that is disobeying the leg a small quarrel early on will lose points, but not as many as an entire test ridden on a stiff and disobedient horse. If the horse lacks impulsion only, the half halt should be tried and a slight shoulder-in—though it will cost points if the judge notices—can be used to unstiffen the horse that becomes tense and anxious on performing in public.

CIRCLES AND SERPENTINES

All circles and serpentines must be round in shape, the right size and performed in the correct places. Asked for a twenty-metre circle at B or E the rider knows that X is the centre and that the boards at E and B are ten metres from X, so he has only to estimate the size on the two quarters where he is crossing the arena. He cannot do this by looking out towards C and A for this would turn his head, shoulders and hips outwards and so reverse the aids. He looks inwards and with one eye on X endeavours to keep precisely the same distance from it as he was at E or B.

A serpentine must always be visualized before it is ridden. The distance of each half circle or loop from the centre line should be paced out and memorized, and the length of the arena must be fairly divided so that the loops are of equal size. The usual three loops in a forty-metre arena work out quite conveniently, for approximately thirteen metres each means that the half-way point of the first half circle will come opposite a quarter marker, the same point on the second half circle will come opposite a half market and on the third circle it will again fall opposite the quarter marker.

The judge will watch each change of bend; he will expect the novice horses to straighten as they cross the centre line and then assume the new bend, and the advanced horses to make that sinuous changeover which only perfect balance, suppleness and a softly flexed jaw can produce.

CANTERING

In a dressage test the canter must be balanced and unhurried, but it must not be slowed until it is in danger of becoming a four time pace. Should the horse strike off on a wrong leg the rider must at once return to the starting pace and strike off again. 'Wrong leg, corrected' will not cost a great many points but left uncorrected it will mean that the movement asked for has not been performed and a nought is all that can be expected. Also the judge's opinion of the rider will be lowered and this means another mark or two off his assessment at the end. These remarks also apply to a disunited canter.

TRANSITIONS

All the transitions must be executed smoothly as the rider's shoulders pass the marker and without visible aids or the horse coming off the bit. The rider must work out how far from the marker he needs to give the aids for a particular movement on a particular horse, for not only are their reaction times different but horses of idle temperament are quick to obey slowing down aids, and the lively animal is more ready to extend than to halt. The sensitive horse needs fair warning of any demand, for he hates to be surprised by aids and, if his rider is unsympathetic, will quickly become upset.

PENALTIES

The use of voice, which includes the clicking of the tongue, costs two points and these are deducted from the movement in which the voice was used. The first time the wrong course is taken two points are deducted, the second time, five, the third, ten and the fourth brings elimination. When a rider loses his way or forgets the test he should ride up to c and let the judge tell him where he went wrong and where he is to start again. It is important not to become flustered, and to be quite clear what one is to do before one restarts. Most judges are extremely helpful to young and novice riders who take the wrong course and will do all they can to sort them out and get them going again.

NERVES

Many horse trial competitors find a dressage test far more of an ordeal than a stiff cross-country course and their anxiety makes it very difficult for their horses, who cannot do their best when carrying a tense rider. Riders should try to be conscious of tenseness and practise relaxing exercises before going in, smiling is a good one as it is impossible to smile and ride with a grimly set jaw.

7

Advanced Jumping

We have taught our horse to jump confidently, uninterfered with by his rider but in the correct shape and from a calm and controlled approach. The aim now is to increase the partnership signals so that the rider, who has walked the course, can give more detailed indications of what lies ahead, but first of all we have to make sure that the hands are not holding the horse back, that the reins are not being used as a slight though continuous brake which would make them less able to pass on special signals.

SURRENDERING THE HANDS

The rider, schooling with short stirrups and the forward seat, practises accelerating into a gallop and coming back into a canter smoothly and calmly but with plenty of impulsion. Then, settling the horse into a steady canter, he slowly slides one hand forward up the neck while he keeps the horse balanced with his legs and seat, but does not drive him forward as he would if he wished to go faster or extend. The schooled horse should not seize the opportunity to increase his pace nor should he collapse on his forehand, he should continue balanced, in the same shape and at the same pace as the rider slowly slides his hand back and resumes contact. After a few strides the rider surrenders the other hand and, when the horse understands what is going on, both hands can be surrendered together.

This exercise is a good one to practise when warming up is almost completed, it keeps both the rider's hands and the horse's mouth sensitive and the fact that the rider can rely on his legs and seat to keep the horse balanced will be of great value when jumping downhill.

HOLDING AND GIVING REINS

Now the rider is in a position to use the actual strength of the rein contact as a signal which, combined with the speed and impulsion of the approach, will if used consistently give the horse a clear idea of what type of fence lies ahead.

The holding rein means 'stand back' the fence ahead is a straight one, has a false ground line, a confusing dip in front of it, is slightly downhill. A holding rein with speed means that the straight fence is also wide though the horse may not be able to see this for himself, as, for instance, a double oxer or a completely parallel poles.

The giving rein means 'take off near' and is used for triples, fences with large ditches on the landing side, and the small brush fence concealing a stretch of water.

Holding and giving are almost too strong words for what the rider should do: He certainly must not hang on or loosen his reins noticeably, they should be small, subtle indications between an experienced rider and horse and should be given during the approach, particularly during the last three strides. Any sudden rein aid on the take-off is liable to confuse the horse, and dropping the hands is often the cause of an experienced horse refusing.

REFUSING

The trained horse knows that jumps are heavy and painful to crash through; he also knows when he has his stride wrong and is going to crash and so, sensibly, he refuses. This is not a disobedience, when turned round he is eager to jump and sails over with the correct stride. There is no point in punishing a horse for this sort of mistake, especially as it may have been the rider's fault that he came in on the wrong stride, and showjumping rules, by allotting less faults to a first refusal than to a knock down, agree that the trained horse's attitude is reasonable.

HALF HALTS

Novice courses should be built to encourage impulsion and a smooth even pace without checks and sharp turns. But the experienced horse can be tested on his ability to shorten and come back to hand as well as on his ability to go forward and extend and, with large fences and a difficult course the half halt becomes essential. This is especially so in combinations where the straight fence follows the spread, where the short distance follows the long, or where the distance does not suit a particular horse and he must be asked to put in a short stride and then sent on with a long one again. It can also be used in between fences if the horse shows signs of going too fast or becoming unbalanced.

One should not check the horse unnecessarily; over-careful riders often rob their horses of all brilliance, and when the half halt is used it must be a true one with the hind legs driven under by the legs and seat. Just using the hands may seem to work for a time but will end with a lack of impulsion, with a horse that 'comes back' but does not 'go on'.

In his first round a rider should make use of the whole ring. This is the same idea as using the whole school at home or the whole arena in a dressage test and shows that the horse is obedient to the inside aids. He must not cut corners unless he is asked to do so.

When it comes to jumping off against the clock it is efficiency of the turns that counts more than the actual speed, and the rider's skill at keeping the horse balanced and on the bit, with his inside hind leg well under him may be the deciding factor in the competition.

ANGLES

When jumping off against the clock it is often a great advantage to take some fences at an angle. We taught our young horse to jump small fences at angles, and now he understands the holding rein we can explain, on approaching a large straight fence, that it is necessary to stand further back on the side nearer the fence than on the other. Spread fences become wider when jumped from an angle, so the rider must always make sure that he is not overfacing his horse by asking for a greater spread than he can cope with.

How much cross-country work a horse intended as a showjumper should do is a difficult question. A little is obviously useful, for banks, ditches and water jumps all appear in the showring, and the slightly uphill or downhill fence can cause trouble among horses that have only jumped on absolutely level ground. But the top class showjumper is now so valuable that he is not usually risked over the more dangerous cross-country fences once his potential is discovered.

Apart from value we have again one of those schooling cross-roads where obedience and independence part company. The showjumping rider with his comparatively few fences, his level ground and his short time in action can plan and execute a much more rider-dominated round than the cross-country rider and so, though cross-country work will improve horses of foxhunter and grade C standards, it is not really recommended for A and JA standards.

RIDING UP AND DOWNHILL

For this work the rider needs to borrow a reasonably steep hillside for two or three days. He also needs four flags or markers and four cavalletti or the equivalent in poles and oil drums. The rider places the flags to mark his course so that he can know for certain whether or not the horse is obeying him.

The idea is to start in the valley, ride uphill for thirty to forty yards, turn at the flag and ride straight along the side or crest of the hill, turn downhill at the next flag and ride absolutely straight down, halting beside the flag at the bottom.

The rider, with short stirrups and his jumping seat, begins at the trot. He rides well forward up the hill, keeps the same even pace along the top and, much more difficult, as he comes down.

Coming down he continues to sit forward—he never leans back—but he can bring his seat closer to the saddle and he remains firmly anchored by the correct position of the lower leg. This correct position of the lower leg is far more important across country than in showjumping and the rider must train himself to keep it at all times. If the leg goes back he will add his

Full of confidence in each other

weight to the horse's forehand, which is dangerous when riding downhill fast or jumping into quarries. If he stiffens his knee and presses the lower leg forward he may feel safer, but he will not be able to use his legs to drive the horse's quarters under him.

With this cross-country work it is a good plan for several riders to practise together. This will allow the horses a breather between turns, enable the riders to give each other advice and moral support and, by providing temptation in the form of a group of horses in the valley, show the rider whether he is in full control coming down.

The first thing to insist upon is that the horse moves at the same even pace uphill, downhill and on the flat, the second that he comes down the hill straight. A horse is much more likely to cross his legs if he comes down crooked or zig-zagging, and coming down crabwise is definitely dangerous. The third thing to insist upon is the halt beside the flag at the bottom.

The whole art of riding downhill safely depends on the ability of the rider to keep his horse balanced by riding forward and driving the hind legs under him. Some riders find it very difficult to make themselves do this, they long to lean back and clutch at the reins, but they must make themselves ride correctly, for, once the idea is recognized and the feeling identified, it all becomes miraculously easy and, provided the horse is reasonably well schooled, going downhill becomes a pleasure instead of the ordeal it is to many riders.

The reckless rider who enjoys a wild disorganised charge is short-sighted if he intends to enter for horse trials, for the fixed fence into a quarry must be treated with respect and jumped in a balanced manner. One should always judge one's performance downhill by whether one would have felt happy to jump into a quarry. If the answer is 'no' one should take the horse straight back and make him come down properly.

The half halt usually corrects the horse which merely becomes unbalanced, but the disobedient horse who decides to take his rider for a gallop should be turned uphill and made to keep going for longer than he likes.

When the horse goes uphill and downhill at the trot he does the same work at the canter, and when this is done well it is a good idea to start the riders at more frequent intervals so that three horses are going round the course at once, each moving at his own pace and with no attempt at racing.

Finally, when the rider feels completely in control, the cavalletti are placed, one in the centre of each slope and the other two making a slightly larger fence halfway along the crest. The rider returns to the trot for his first attempt, and if he *has* been holding back with the reins he will find jumping down rather unnerving, but, if he has the horse going properly there will be no problems and he can ride round at the canter.

QUARRIES AND DROPS

When horse and rider are confident over cavalletti downhill they must look around for some larger fences, but since jumping downhill is a strain on the horse's legs, it should not be over-practised. Disused quarries are usually fairly easy to borrow, and, if it is possible to build some permanent jumps, try to arrange them so that there are alternative routes in and out. This will stop the horse growing over-confident and make him wait for your instructions.

Large downhill fences must always be ridden with holding reins as the horse has to be encouraged to stand back, the rider who collapses on his neck or drops his hands at the last moment drives the horse under the fence and makes it almost impossible to take off.

There are always arguments over drop fences. Some riders insist on leaning back and letting the reins slip through their fingers. This works all right when there is a long way to go before the next fence and so plenty of time to regain the seat, pick up the reins and put the horse back on the bit. If there is another fence immediately, the rider risks a run out or, by leaving the whole negotiation of it to the poor horse, who hasn't walked the course—a fall.

The thinking behind the leaning back is that if the horse pecks on landing you will be less likely to shoot over his head, but the *correct* forward seat firmly anchored by a correct leg position gives a firm seat and control at the same time.

Most drops are situated in tricky situations and are therefore taken slowly, the exception is a hedge with a drop out in the open on a galloping course, but even here a slight slowing down, a half halt, will warn the horse that there is something a little extra ahead and the rider should not ride on with total abandon unless the drop is such that it would become much less severe if the horse landed well out in the next field.

BANKS

The sleeper-faced Irish bank and the staircase are frequently met in horse trials, and so the horse must be given some experience of them. The simplest way of showing him what he is expected to do is to ask an older horse to provide a lead.

The staircase just needs agility, but if a horse goes to a competition without having seen one before he may stop for a look and collect a refusal.

Large banks terrify some young horses. They jump up, and then finding an abyss all round them are so overcome with vertigo and panic they refuse to jump down. So if you can find one about three feet high for your first attempt it will save a lot of problems.

Approaching at the trot and then cantering on the last few strides, the rider has to remember that he is about to make two jumps and that the moment the horse is on the bank he must be ridden forward and off. Allowing horses to 'dwell' is dangerous, especially on the square artificial bank, as they can fall off backwards and sideways. The rider must have his whip, heel and voice ready, as well as his usual aids, and he uses the lot if the horse shows any sign of dwelling or dithering.

Ditches and poles on the landing side should not be introduced until the horse is completely confident and jumping on and off with plenty of impulsion.

In horse trials banks are usually taken fast unless the siting is tricky, but out hunting they are generally taken slowly as unexpected hazards may lurk on the landing side.

Horses brought up away from water often hate the thought of jumping it and some, especially those with Arab blood, object to getting their feet wet by walking through puddles.

If one has a horse like this one must never lose an opportunity to take him through shallow water with a hard bottom. Riding through boggy places which clutch at his hoofs and seem to be sucking him down will only make him more nervous. Riding directly after storms is a very good practice. Long rides can be made to places where there are fords, and friendships must be struck up with those who own brooks; but, most important of all, one must dig a water jump of one's own.

I once had a horse called Rosebay who really hated water, but I cured him by these methods and he went on to become an open horse trial horse and only once did I have any trouble over water in a competition.

When making your own water jump, the site needs to be on level ground near a water trough or tap and with plenty of room for a straight approach and landing. The face of the jump should be twelve feet wide and the width across about ten feet. Mark the area you have measured out with pegs. Dig up the turf in squares and pile. Dig out about six inches of earth. If you can acquire a quarter of a yard of builder's sand spread half of this on the dug out area, otherwise rake smooth and remove stones. Acquire a sheet of heavy duty polythene not less than sixteen feet by sixteen. Spread this on the dug out area. Acquire two stout twelve-foot poles, wind the over-lap of the polythene on the take-off and landing sides round these poles, and wedge them tightly against the surrounding turf. Secure the overlap on the other two sides by covering it with earth and turf. If you have got the sand, put the rest on top of the polythene. Fill with water.

With a pole over the centre or a two-foot brush fence on the take-off side this will make a very useful jump, and I recommend some sort of wing as this saves quarrelling with the horse who offers a compromise by jumping the corner. Jumping into water can be arranged by moving the brush forward about three feet so that the horse popping over it from the trot will land in the water. This is not good for the polythene. The really water-shy horse who refuses to approach the jump at all must be tempted in by kindness. A pair of gumboots, a bucket of the horse's favourite food and several hours of free time are the only answer.

DITCHES

I have already described the Irish method of dealing with ditch-haters; the next step is to dig your own small ditch and enlarge it week by week as the horse gains confidence. Leads from experienced horses are also a great help, especially over strange ditches found out hacking. These horse phobias are very irritating but they are never improved by riders who also become upset, nor are they cured by lost tempers and beatings.

OTHER FENCES

Jumping the corner of a triangle pen should be practised at home and not tried out for the first time in a horse trial. Very narrow fences, such as hunting gates, with wings turned back and sloping away from the approach, water troughs and hay racks with their false ground lines, are all met in competition and the rider will feel much more confident if he knows his horse will do them.

Dark woods should be jumped into at every opportunity. Some horses are horrified by them and even bold horses prefer to jump out of a wood rather than in.

8

Solving Tack Problems

The less tack the better. The well-made, well-schooled horse can manage with just a saddle and a bridle. Dangling festoons of martingales, flapping saddle cloths and, worst of all, pink foam rubber bathmats serve no useful purpose and make the horse look a mess.

THE BRIDLE

A snaffle bridle, and most horses go well in a thick, jointed bit, is the only possible choice for a young unspoilt horse, but do make sure the bridle fits. Don't be misled into buying a complete cob size bridle if your fifteen-hand horse has a pony size mouth and needs a horse size browband. Buy the parts in the right sizes and make the bridle up.

The double bridle is *not* an extra severe brake for a horse that won't stop. It should only be used on schooled horses for the purpose of producing a finer and more elegant performance and it does enable a skilled rider to give even lighter and more invisible aids than the snaffle.

REINS

For adventurous riding reins should be covered with rubber as this will give a grip if there is a sudden downpour in the middle of your round and you cannot stop to put on string gloves. Reins for jumping must not be so long that they entangle themselves round your foot when you ride with short stirrups. If they do they must be shortened, but a knot by the buckle will do as a temporary measure. Plaited nylon reins are suitable for gymkhanas but not for more serious riding.

A saddle has to fit the rider as well as the horse. It should have a deep central seat and not slide the rider back towards the cantle as old-fashioned saddles were inclined to do. When the stirrups are short the rider's knees must still be able to rest on the saddle flaps. If they are sliding about on the horse's shoulder the rider will never develop a firm jumping seat.

Too much stuffing and too much padding under the knee gives a feeling of being divorced from the horse, but a knee roll helps to produce the rock-like seat all cross-country riders desire.

GIRTHS

The best girth used to be the folded leather type, but the nylon string girth has proved itself tough and durable and has made girth galls a rarity instead of the common lot of all young and unfit horses.

Breastplates A breastplate prevents the saddle sliding back. If a saddle does slide back it often frightens the horse into hysteria; he bucks wildly, the saddle goes under his stomach, the rider has a horrible fall under the trampling feet and the horse may gallop for miles in an effort to escape from the upside-down saddle. So all herring-gutted horses with powerful shoulders should wear breastplates, especially when hunting for, as they lose weight and their stomachs run up, there is less and less to stop the girth slipping.

Three-day Event horses also suffer a weight loss during the competition and unless they have extra well-sprung ribs they should wear breastplates, in fact it is a useful piece of equipment for any cross-country rider.

Steeplechasers sometimes wear webbing breastplates, but the leather kind that fastens round the girth, round the neck and buckles on the D's of the saddle is more correct and probably more comfortable for hunters and eventers.

Safety girths For Point-to-points and Three-day Events most competitors add a narrow webbing surcingle which passes over the seat of the saddle and buckles on to itself. This saves the situation should the girth straps break away from the saddle, and is a good safety measure where there is to be violent exertion at speed.

WEIGHT CLOTHS

If you enter for a competition which requires that you ride at a special weight, weigh yourself and your saddle. If you are not heavy enough you will have to buy a weight cloth to go under your saddle and thin slices of lead to slide into its pockets. When the rider weighs in after a competition he is allowed to add his bridle and whip if he cannot make the weight, but they should not be counted in beforehand as he may lose weight during the round.

NUMNAHS

Numnahs are needed by horses with sensitive backs. They are usually saddle-shaped, padded affairs or made of felt or sheepskin. Horses that have had back trouble, the thin-skinned, cold-backed and recently clipped all find them a comfort, and also horses that are allergic to saddle soap.

A famous vet once told me that a jumping saddle concentrates a rider's weight on such a small area of the horse's back that he recommended numnahs for all jumpers.

CORRECTIVE TACK

Some tack is designed to prevent certain problems, and it is well to be clear in one's mind what one is trying to do before one uses it, and to make sure that one understands the correct adjustments.

DROP NOSEBANDS

The aim of these nosebands is to prevent the horse opening his mouth *wide* and so evading the bit. The plain drop noseband is allowed in all novice and Pony Club dressage tests; the grakle is allowed in combined training competitions at the time of writing and will be allowed in Pony Club competitions from 1974.

Correct adjustment is very important, and they are often worn too low on the nose which interferes with the horse's breathing. The front part of the noseband should be as high as possible while permitting the back strap to fit into the chin-groove, and the back strap must *never* be pulled up tight. We want to stop the horse opening his mouth wide, we do not want to stop him flexing his jaw for this will give him a hard mouth. So there must be room for three fingers in the back strap.

PELHAMS

Pelham bits are suitable for horses which have been spoiled by bad riding, particularly those which carry their heads too high as both reins work the curb chain, the top less than the lower. This means that there is always a downward action on the head-carriage. Obviously this makes them bad bits for horses that are already too much on their forehands or which overbend and quite unsuitable for the most usual wearers of pelhams, fat little ponies which pull with their heads *down*.

The vulcanite pelham is a kind bit and particularly suitable for a horse that is carrying his head too high because he is frightened of his mouth and whose rider cannot afford the three months needed to re-school him quietly in a snaffle. Pelhams may not be worn in Pony Club dressage tests; double bridles are allowed but of course you do not qualify for the three extra points given for wearing a snaffle.

CURB CHAINS

I am always being surprised by finding otherwise efficient riders with their curb chains incorrectly put on and causing their horses discomfort if not actual pain.

The chain should be hooked on the off side while the rider, standing on the near, twists it away from the horse's chin until it is absolutely flat. He then hooks the first link on the near side hook downwards and whichever link he choses for the adjustment—usually the third if the curb chain fits the horse—upwards. If he has got it right the whole chain presents a hard flat surface with no individual links able to dig into the horse's chin groove, and the top edge of the chain is further from the chin groove than the lower edge. This is very important, as when a feel is taken on the lower rein the curb chain will press flat and comfortably in the groove and not hurt him by pressing with one of its edges. Any rider using a curb chain should always check that it is working correctly by feeling the lower rein and watching its action before mounting. The other point he checks is the tightness.

When the reins are not in use the bit cheeks lie along the line of the horse's mouth; when the reins are felt and the cheeks move back the curb chain advances on the chin groove and it should come into action and begin to press when the cheeks are at an angle of forty-five degrees to the mouth. If the double bridle is being worn for appearance's sake rather than use, as in a showing class, it can be a link or two looser; but it should never be tighter,

Correctly-fitted curb chain

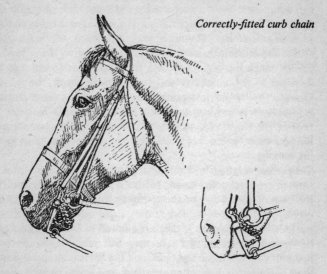

for the whole idea of the curb chain is to provide a time lag. If the horse is attentive to the bit and obeys the lightest touch the curb chain does not work: it only comes into action when the rider has asked for a couple of seconds and it ceases to work the moment the horse flexes his jaw. A really tight curb chain will teach the horse to pull as he will have to try to deaden the pain it is causing him.

There is a difference in the fitting of a curb chain on a double bridle and a pelham. With a double bridle it passes *below* the rings of the bridoon and on a pelham it passes *through* the rings on the cheek pieces. Also, a lip strap is always worn with a double bridle but is optional with a pelham.

MARTINGALES

Martingales are an admission of bad manners and so they are not allowed in dressage tests and must not be worn in showing classes.

Standing martingales are useful on young horses inclined to throw up their heads unexpectedly and bang their riders on the nose, and many trainers put them on for over-exciting occasions such as a first hunt. The horse must on no account be strapped down; the martingale must only come into action if the head is carried much too high. To check the adjustment detach the end fastened to the noseband and turn it back across the horse's shoulder; it should just reach the withers. A standing martingale cannot improve the horse's head-carriage; it is there to protect the rider and, as it is a nuisance and catches on gate latches, there is no point in wearing one unless one needs protection.

The running martingale Running martingales are a useful form of control on unschooled or spoiled horses and are widely used by the present generation of showjumping riders, but they must be correctly adjusted so that they only come into use if the horse puts his head in the air. If they are allowed to exercise a constant downward action on the rein they will produce an overbent horse. If they are much too tight, and the horse is strapped down, they will destroy his action, carriage and spirit as well. Some experts use two reins on a snaffle and fit the running martingale to the lower one. They should not be used with double bridles or pelhams, as the combination is too severe.

Stops, small pieces of leather fitted to the reins, should be used with reins that are buckled or stud-billeted to the bit as the martingale rings can catch and jam on them. This is very frightening to the horse, who suddenly finds his head tied down and may panic, crashing backwards into people or cars or other horses.

The Irish martingale was once in fairly general use, but it serves no useful purpose in modern riding and is rarely seen.

Boots and bandages may not be worn in dressage tests so the horse trial rider has the tiresome task of putting them on between phases. One thing which every rider should try to learn from the experience of others is not to oil the hoofs before putting on overreach boots.

As with tack the less the better; less to leave behind, less to put on, less to fall off during your round. If my horse overreached I would see the blacksmith before I bought the boots, for quite a small adjustment, the setting back of a hind shoe, can often cure the trouble. Since tiredness and deep going are two contributory factors, the fit horse and the thoughtful rider are in less need of boots than their opposites.

Bandages support the tendons and older horses or horses which have suffered sprains in the past are often advised by their vets to wear them. Some riders misunderstand the point of bandages and put on washed-out crepe which, having no elasticity in it, does more to stop the circulation than anything else. Springy bandages must be put on tightly, but always over gamgee or some suitable substitute; the tapes must be knotted on the outside of the cannon bone, never on the tendons and with reef knots, not bows which will be pulled undone by bracken and brambles. For any important competition the ends of the tapes should be sewn as well as tied.

Brushing boots are useful for the thin-skinned horse which finishes every cross-country scratched and chipped, as well as those that brush.

STUDS

Jumping studs are a bore. You have to remember to ask the blacksmith to make the stud holes when he fits the shoes and you have to put them in and take them out on the showground; they are much larger than the mordex stud and the horse must not wear them in the box, stable or on the road. However, they do make all the difference in the world to the way you can ride on slippery wet or slippery dry ground and anyone who intends to ride to win, anyone who means to cut corners and take chances,

must have them. The usual arrangement is one stud in the outside
heel of each foot and you will need a 'tap' for clearing the thread,
some cotton wool for stuffing in the hole when you take the
stud out, some implement for picking the cotton wool out when
you want to put the stud in and a spanner for tightening and
loosening.

SPURS

Blunt spurs are worn to give boots an elegant look or in an
attempt to persuade a reasonably schooled, but naturally idle,
horse to obey a lighter aid. They should not be worn on young
horses or by inexperienced riders.

Sharp spurs should only be worn by dressage experts on highly
schooled horses in order to maintain obedience to the lightest
possible aid. The rowels may look imposing but they should be
filed down so that when they protrude from the neck of the spur
to touch the horse they cannot give him more than the merest
prick.

WHIPS

No good rider ever rides without a whip and he trains himself to
carry it and use it in either hand. Satisfactory whips can be cut
from the hedge or wood, but I like to see them bound round with
insulating tape at the top, especially for jumping when the rider
can jab himself in the face if the horse makes an awkward jump.

Long whips are best for schooling, as they can be used without the need to take the hand off the rein, but no whip of more
than thirty inches in length may be carried in a jumping
competition.

CHECKING TACK

A broken stirrup leather, a broken rein, a broken girth can all
lose a competition and waste weeks of careful training and
preparation. So they must be checked and replaced or repaired
at the end of every season or holidays.

Stirrup leathers should always be re-stitched at the beginning
of the horse trial season. The saddler should be asked to check
that they are the same length, for the one that is used for mounting

generally stretches more than the other. Some authorities advise changing them over at regular intervals to prevent this, but the competition rider knows that a stirrup leather used always on the same side acquires a twist and automatically returns a lost stirrup to the searching foot, and this is worth the trouble of dealing with any amount of uneven stretching.

9

Reaching Stardom

No one can get to the top without some talent. The best horse and trainer, a family prepared to offer every assistance, cannot make a star of a rider who has no star qualities. Of course a good instructor, a clever, bold horse, a helpful family background give the rider a wonderful start and make the way to success a lot easier. For those without them, single-mindedness will be required in direct ratio to this lack of opportunity.

To school horses one needs love, understanding and patience. To be a first-class competition rider requires courage, the will to win, quick judgement, toughness and a staying power to drive yourself on when exhausted and prevents you from going to pieces when things go wrong. Then, because there is so much talent at the top and the competition is so fierce, there is the essential but dull behind-the-scene work which gives the mediocre rider an edge on his equals and makes the star almost unbeatable.

LONG-TERM PLANNING

Under the long-term heading come the things which have to be done once a year or at the beginning of the season.

The ordinary horse needs a yearly check for teeth and worms The older horse, the horse that is to compete in horse trials or other strenuous events such as the Golden Horseshoe Ride, will need his heart and lungs tested as well. No one wants a horse to drop dead under them and this does occasionally happen.

As all rules are changed from time to time it is never safe to assume that they are the same as they were last year. Nothing is more bitter than being eliminated after a good round because one was unaware that a new rule had been introduced. New rule books should be acquired from the British Horse Society, the British Showjumping Association or the Pony Club, and last year's books thrown away.

Check all stitching and possible breakage points on your tack at the beginning of the season and before every event. All the careful training, all the talent and star qualities, can be wasted when a rein or stirrup leather or girth break in the middle of a round.

Remember that the horse cannot be relaxed unless the rider is relaxed, and make the organization as easy as possible for yourself. This is particularly important at horse trials when the brain has to remember a dressage test and two courses and so should be kept free of minor worries.

One way to do this is to acquire a large box or trunk in which all grooming tools, bandages, boots, studs, sewing outfit, first-aid kit, spare reins, string gloves, everything you need is packed for every competition. A list of all the things which should be in the box is made and attached to the lid and this makes it very easy to check, even on those panic-stricken mornings when everything has gone wrong. Another list should be made of all necessary gear not in the box, from polo-necked sweater to haynet; and including the two objects most commonly left behind, the rider's hat and the horse's girth. White nylon girths are always forgotten because they have been put to dry in the kitchen or airing cupboard.

A hat that fits is essential, and for Pony Club competitions, in which a rider is now eliminated if he continues to jump having lost his hat, a hat strap is a good investment. The male sex really needs the detachable sort which can be removed and put in the pocket for dressage tests and prize-givings, and other occasions when hats have to be taken off in a hurry.

The crash helmet offers the best protection and there is now a move to allow them in competitions other than horse trials. If this comes about a dark blue or black silk will have to be worn.

When entering for a large number of shows, some sort of file or system is needed. The schedules must be kept, the classes marked and, if the horse has to be declared, the date and time of this should be noted.

Riders must not be greedy, they must allow time for the horse to rest and recuperate between competitions. Many a good horse becomes stale and finally takes to refusing simply because he is being worked to death; not physically perhaps, but through the stress and strain and tension of shows and the travelling involved. Jumping large fences is tiring both mentally and physically. A stiff cross-country course is a severe test of a horse's stamina, courage and judgement, and one that he should not be asked to make too often.

Then there is the question of meals. Owing to the small size of his stomach the horse finds it quite difficult to catch up on missed meals, and the rider must consider this when he is tempted to enter for show after show.

Besides rest days an occasional complete change is needed. A twenty-five mile hack through little-known territory will do the jaded showjumper a great deal of good, for the relaxed state of physical tiredness is entirely different from the exhausted state of mental tiredness brought about by travelling and competitions.

SHORT-TERM PLANNING

When concerned with the requirements of a particular competition read the schedule carefully, and if anything special is wanted make sure that you and your horse have practised it adequately.

If entering for the cross-country phase of a tetrathlon, for instance, there will be a gate to open and shut and slip rails to cope with. If you can persuade someone to time your efforts you can work out the fastest routine and, at the same time, you can teach your horse that though you are approaching the fence fast, if you shout 'Whoa' and take your feet out of the stirrups he is to stop and not jump. Misunderstandings over slip rails can occur and you do not want the horse to jump with you half off; nor do you want him to stop at rails in ordinary cross-country events and wait for you to take them down.

When entering for combined training or horse trials, always check which test is being used and learn it carefully. This is something that becomes easier with practice, though carrying several different tests in one's head and perhaps performing two of them on the same day does present problems.

Some people learn tests by sitting up in bed and proceeding round the plan of the arena on the back of the test sheet with a finger-tip moving at the appropriate pace, others have to walk round the actual arena. It is better not to involve the horse in your learning processes, for if he knows the test too well he will begin to anticipate your aids and a good judge should notice and remove marks. So, when mounted, carry out individual movements as often as you like but only ride the whole test straight through occasionally.

TRAVEL WEAR

Small ponies seem to bear charmed lives; they whirl about in cattle trucks with no protective clothing and emerge unscathed. But horses are more accident prone and generally need some wrapping up. How much depends on the value of the horse, the importance of the competition, the distance to be travelled, the time of year and the owner's nerves.

It varies from the hunter who travels to a meet already tacked up, a rug thrown over his saddle and a tail bandage all that has to be taken off on arrival; to the knee caps, hock boots and poll protectors of the flying horse. The intermediate dress of well-padded stable bandages, rug and tail bandage is probably enough for most horses, though the horse which sits on his tail will need a tail guard as well as a bandage.

ARRIVAL

On arrival at the ground a visit to the secretary's tent to collect your number or numbers should be made, and it is also as well to enquire if the official times still stand or whether cancellations have upset the timetable. It is very disconcerting to have an angry

113

collecting steward bellowing at you to go in hours before you expect to be called.

WALKING THE CROSS-COUNTRY

It is very important to walk the course calmly and carefully, and it is often worth visiting the ground the evening before the event to give yourself plenty of time. Short courses of one mile can be done on the day, but two miles and upwards takes rather a lot out of the rider just before a competition.

Choose your companions carefully. The over-talkative will distract your attention, the nervous may put you off.

Look at the plan first and then set off for the start. Always go through the start and then take the exact path you intend to ride on your horse. This will ensure that you notice patches of bad going or natural hazards.

The first jump should be fairly easy, but if it is not, if there is any trick about it, if the run is very short or it is half-hidden round a bend, take no chances at all. Approach absolutely square, slowly but full of impulsion and use stronger than usual aids to draw the horse's attention to it.

As you come to each fence try to see it from the horse's point of view as he approaches without having walked the course. Notice if it appears large or small or easy and whether the ground line is true, and then, having reached the fence you will know if there is anything of which you should warn him. A ditch on the landing side—push on. A downhill landing and another fence immediately—slow up and pop. A sharp turn on landing—go back and choose a helpful angle of approach, and fix it in your mind with a landmark.

DITCHES

Do not waste time looking into the bottoms of ditches, tiger and elephant traps. If the horse approaches at the correct pace he will clear them automatically. They demand no extra effort unless they increase the width of the jump beyond the normal take-off and landing areas. But if you are worrying about them the horse will sense this and may feel he ought to stop for a look.

114

DOWNHILL FENCES

You have taught your horse to jump downhill correctly so have confidence in your training and do not allow yourself to be put off by fellow competitors who wail and groan. And if it is slippery, well, you have studs in front and behind and you know to take the fence slowly and with a holding rein.

UPHILL FENCES

If this is sited after a long or steep uphill gallop you must settle where you intend to offer your horse a breather. You will need a lot of impulsion, so slow up some way from the fence and be riding hard by the time you get there. If you arrive on a breathless horse, you risk a refusal or even a fall and in Pony Club horse trials, where time is not of much importance, it would be foolish not to give the horse a chance to ease up.

WATER JUMPS

Before a stream or brook you also need to pick a half-halting point. The usual hell-for-leather approach of the inexperienced is always started too far away, and though it may look impressive the horse actually reaches the water with dying impulsion and the result is often a refusal followed by a loud splash. The rider should half halt, give the horse the normal run for a triple, and arrive on a lengthening stride and with increasing impulsion.

SPLASHES AND PONDS

If the water is to be jumped into, try to imagine how it will look to your horse who has not read its official description. Is it obvious that he is meant to jump in; or could he mistake it for an enormous brook which you, in a fit of madness, are asking him to jump over? If he could make a mistake, work out your approach with care. The slow approach he associates with a 'pop' may be the answer or coming at it from an angle may make it plain that he is to get in, not leap over.

ALTERNATIVE FENCES

Which of two alternative fences you take depends very much on your horse's stride and ability. One might suit a short-striding horse, the other the horse with scope. With an inexperienced horse always choose the easier, even if it means a slight loss of time. When riding to win on an experienced horse take the time-saver, unless time does not count, or it is a fence that your horse particularly dislikes. Where there are alternative pens, choose the one with the knockdownable 'in' and the solid 'out'; most horses are more likely to flatten or be careless over the out.

HORIZON FENCES

These fences are cleverly placed on the crests of hills and can give the horse the impression that he is jumping into space. This last minute fear can cause an unexpected refusal. They should be ridden a little slower than usual, as the extra second will give the horse the chance to see the hill below. Also, the fact that you are obviously attentive and not riding wildly will give him confidence that you know what you are about.

MULTIPLE PROBLEMS

If a fence presents the horse with so many different problems that he cannot assimilate them between catching sight of the fence and reaching the point of take-off he will almost certainly refuse. Imagine a right-angled pen, the first fence on the horizon, framed above by the bough of a tree and with an uneven take-off. Obviously if the rider comes at this sort of jump fast the horse will feel overwhelmed with problems, in the same way as a car driver does arriving at a strange roundabout. There comes a moment when the motorist cannot assimilate it all fast enough and he must either stop or drive round the roundabout and come back for another look. In fact he has to refuse or run out, and so does the horse for exactly the same reason.

The answer is a slow approach in order to allow the horse maximum inspection time, a lot of thought on how to make the particular fence as easy as possible, and very alert riding to deal with any of the horse's last minute doubts.

Very often these fences are small and can easily be jumped from a trot, but if you have doubts about what is best ask a friend to go and watch a few horses over the fence and then to come back and report to you at the start about the most successful speeds and methods.

COFFINS

Coffins are usually a combination of a downhill fence, a large ditch about one stride away, followed immediately by another fence. They cause a lot of refusals, especially among riders who come in too fast. The horse's fear is that he is going to land too near the ditch to be able to take off, and will then slide into its probably bottomless depths. And of course if the distance is short and the horse jumps with scope the faster the rider approaches the more likely this is to happen. In fact the coffin is a test of whether the rider has taught his horse to jump slowly but with great impulsion when needed.

DARK WOODS

Even on a trained horse the rider should always ride a little harder than usual when jumping from bright sunshine into a gloomy wood, as there is just a chance of a refusal.

Shadows and sunshine sometimes play tricks with fences, giving them false ground lines or producing other optical illusions. If a fence that caused no trouble early in the day begins to pile up refusals and faults towards evening, inspect the going. If it is not unduly cut up, the trouble may be due to the changed position of the sun. If it is, try to work out what the other horses are doing wrong and then help yours to avoid the error. Taking a fence at an angle will save jumping straight into a setting sun.

FINISHES AND FLAGS

Always take a careful look at the finish and make sure you know exactly which two objects you are to pass between.

Flags are normally red and white, and the rider must always leave red ones on his right and white ones on his left. Over the fences this is generally obvious for one simply jumps between them, but when a turning flag is placed out in the middle of a field the rider must take great care to memorise its position and which way round he is supposed to go. It is infuriating to be eliminated for missing out a turning flag, but it usually happens to everyone once in a lifetime.

Yellow direction markers are simply to help the rider to find his way, and may be passed on either side. If a competitor is in any doubt about a flag he should always consult an official.

Here, starts and finishes need even more attention, for correcting your mistake can cost you a refusal, and if you have taken the first fence or galloped gaily out of the ring before correcting it, you will be eliminated. As you inspect the start remind yourself that you must wait for the signal to start, or at the end of a perfect round you may hear the announcer saying regretfully that you were eliminated for starting before the bell.

Some top-class riders, having taught themselves to stride exactly thirty-six inches, walk the course allowing four of their strides to one of the horse's, and check even the unrelated fences to see whether the horse is going to find good or bad distances between them. If from landing to take-off they find they have a half stride, or six feet, over they then decide whether to come in a little faster than usual and spread it among the longer strides they will be taking, or a little slower so that it can collect a few more inches and become a stride in its own right.

But most riders content themselves with pacing out the combinations. They walk the exact route they intend to take noting any awkwardly-placed fences, and any difficult corners where they will have to work hard to keep the horse balanced. They decide on their approach to individual fences; where they must take off near a fence, where they must stand back; where to ride carefully because the fence falls easily or could give the horse a wrong impression of its height or width; where to ride hard because their horse dislikes that type of jump. Then they look at the fences in relation to each other. They see that the triple follows a sharp turn and if they come round unbalanced they will be in trouble, so they decide to go right down to the ring ropes and give themselves plenty of room. There is no hurry in the first round. And after the water jump there are some high, straight rails which will cause trouble to the horses that are really going on so the water must be taken a little slower than normal. A quick half halt

118

on landing should collect the horse enough before he is sent on at the rails.

Combinations must be paced out carefully, and with a treble this will probably have to be done more than once before the rider makes his decision. The decision of whether to lengthen or shorten, whether to go for one long stride or two very short ones, must be made with knowledge of the particular horse, but, as a general rule, the less checking the better. Though here again the compact horse will accept checking better than the horse that stands over a lot of ground, is long from hip to hock, and so finds it more difficult to bring his hind legs under him.

If there is a shortened course for the jump-off, and it is against the clock, the rider should walk round again if possible. He now has to find the shortest way round and work out which fences will pay him to jump at an angle. Some angles put you wrong for the following fence and are therefore pointless. It is the horse which can make neat, tight turns without coming off the bit and the rider who sees that he can cut inside the unused fence, who win against the clock. The wild galloper loses on his wide turns what he gains by speed, and if he comes off the bit and flattens he is liable to bring down a fence as well.

Obviously, exactly how you ride in a jump-off depends on the position you have drawn. The early riders must try for fast clears while the last rider may only need a careful clear, or he goes in knowing that only a fantastic speed will enable him to win. The early rider who knocks a fence should always increase speed at once, for if there are not many clears the fastest four faults may well be in the money.

THE DRESSAGE TEST

One does not walk the dressage, but an inexperienced competitor should always take a look at the arena and see which way round it is laid out. If one has been practising at home with c to the south, it can be disconcerting to find it laid to the north and it may take a few minutes to re-orientate oneself. These should not be the first few minutes in the arena.

How long you ride-in before a competition depends on the horse. Older horses usually need less work, excitable horses need a lot. Lazy horses need a little very energetic work to wake them up and get their hind legs under them.

The competitor has to find out what suits the horse by experience. If he makes a note of how long he rides-in and the result after each show, he will soon find what produces the horse's best performance.

The first ten minutes of riding-in should just be exercise. To demand specific movements from an excited horse straight out of a box is asking for trouble, he should be ridden round at the walk and trot and allowed to look about him. If his back is up and he seems to have grown to about twenty hands at precisely the same moment as the rider's legs have turned to jelly, he must be exercised hard, but still at the trot. The rider probably feels an irresistible desire to hang on to the reins and hold the horse back into a jog, but he must control himself and find a quiet corner where he can ride the horse round and round a school-sized area, riding him forward, really making him take exercise, until his back relaxes and he settles down.

When the horse is relaxed the rider can begin to school, but he must have it clearly in his mind what he is trying to achieve. One sees inexperienced competitors cantering vague and sleepy circles as though hoping for magical effects. But it is not the circle; it is obedience, impulsion and suppleness that matter, and the rider should practise whatever best produces those three things in his particular horse, and include some energetic shoulder in at the trot.

All riders have nerves, but some control them better than others. To be a star, you have to stop them affecting your horse. Jelly legs and clutching hands will turn the usually sensible animal into a pulling, bucking maniac. The rider who tenses and becomes irritable will make his horse tense and worried too; he will lead off on the wrong leg, his ears will be back and the relaxed swing of his trot will vanish. The rider who feels that things are going wrong must make a determined effort to relax himself, ride with reins in one hand, look round at the tree-tops and stop demanding that the horse goes perfectly, for he cannot be expected to go one bit better than he does at home.

As the time for a dressage test approaches the rider must remove all forbidden tack and bandages and abandon his whip. As the time for a jumping competition draws near the rider checks his studs and girth and that he has a whip of the right length.

Practice jumps For cross-country the practice jump is just a matter of warming up, unless the competitor has found some strange fence on the course and is hastily attempting to build a replica. The showjumper should be asked to jump something more formidable when he has warmed up over several easy fences; a parallel perhaps, for then the rider can check that he is standing back and has impulsion.

At a horse trial the horse will need several more practice jumps before his showjumping round, for the longer, lower shape and faster pace of the cross-country horse must be changed for the more collected form of the showjumper.

For the last few minutes before entering the ring a horse should be kept on the move and not allowed to fall asleep or to keep amiable company with other horses, for one makes for an unbalanced and disorganised start and the other for nappiness.

STAR BEHAVIOUR

Being in the public eye means that one's faults are magnified and it is necessary to exercise extra self-control if one is not to be disliked by the public and loathed by one's fellow competitors. This is especially so when you first begin to win at local shows, and the early rungs of the ladder to stardom will be very hard if it is not realized that losers want to hate winners and search hard for reasons to do so.

Be publicly nice to your horse and give him the lion's share of the credit. It is true you trained him, but you could not have won if he was a coward or without talent.

Be polite to the judges even if you disagree with them. You are entitled to object, but it must be done in a quiet and dignified manner.

Be pleasant to the other competitors whether you win or lose; try not to sound boastful or superior.

Riding better and better

Don't swear at anyone, horse, fence judges or parents. It leaves a bad taste in the mouth of those who hear, and if you get a bad reputation you will not be wanted in teams, Junior European, Pony Club, Riding Club or the Olympics, however well you ride.

When you lose through some silly mistake of your own or on the part of the horse, do not take it out on those around you; of course you will feel fed up after all that work and training but keep it to yourself, and let it harden into determination never to make the same mistake again.

All this may sound pompous, but some people are spoiled by success, and it would be a great pity if in the act of riding better and better my readers became less likeable characters.